A Dog's Life

A Dog's Life

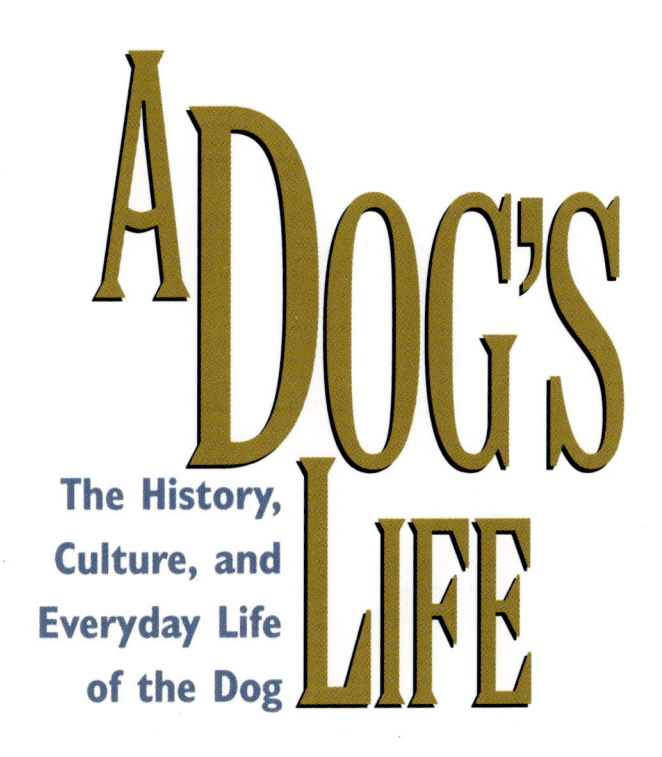

The History, Culture, and Everyday Life of the Dog

Amy Shojai

FRIEDMAN/FAIRFAX
PUBLISHERS

A FRIEDMAN/FAIRFAX BOOK

© 1994 by Michael Friedman Publishing Group, Inc.

All rights reserved. No part of this publication may be reproduced, stored in a retrieval system, or transmitted, in any form or by any means, electronic, mechanical, photocopying, recording, or otherwise, without prior written permission from the publisher.

Library of Congress Cataloging-in-Publication Data

Shojai, Amy, 1956-
   [Dog companion]
   A dog's life : the history, culture, and everyday life of the dog / Amy Shojai.
     p.   cm.
   "Originally published as The dog companion"--T.p. verso.
   Includes bibliographical references (p.   ) and index.
   ISBN 1-56799-112-2 (paperback)
   1. Dogs.   I. Title.
SF426.S545   1994
599.74'442--dc20   94-9540
                                                                                        CIP

Editor: Elizabeth Viscott Sullivan
Art Director: Devorah Levinrad
Designer: Ed Noriega
Photography Editors: Anne K. Price and Emilya Naymark

Originally published as *The Dog Companion*

Page 2 photograph © George Munday/Leo de Wys
Page 3 photograph © Sally Anne Thompson/Animal Photography, London
Page 46 photograph © Scala/Art Resource, New York

Output by Sarabande
Printed and bound in China by L.Rex Printing Company Limited

For bulk purchases and special sales, please contact:
Friedman/Fairfax Publishers
15 West 26th Street
New York, NY 10010
212/685-6610 FAX 212/685-1307

DEDICATION

This book is dedicated to Nobody's Dog

ACKNOWLEDGMENTS

I'd like to thank the many dog lovers and organizations whose expertise helped
make researching the manuscript a joy, especially the
Sherman Public Library, Sherman, Texas, and Karen Elwood.
My deepest appreciation goes to my husband, Mahmoud Shojai,
whose understanding means more than I can say; my parents,
Phil and Mary Monteith, who always believed in me;
and Fafnir, whose "floffy mooch" says it all!
I would also like to thank Christopher Shaw of the
Los Angeles County Museum of Natural History.

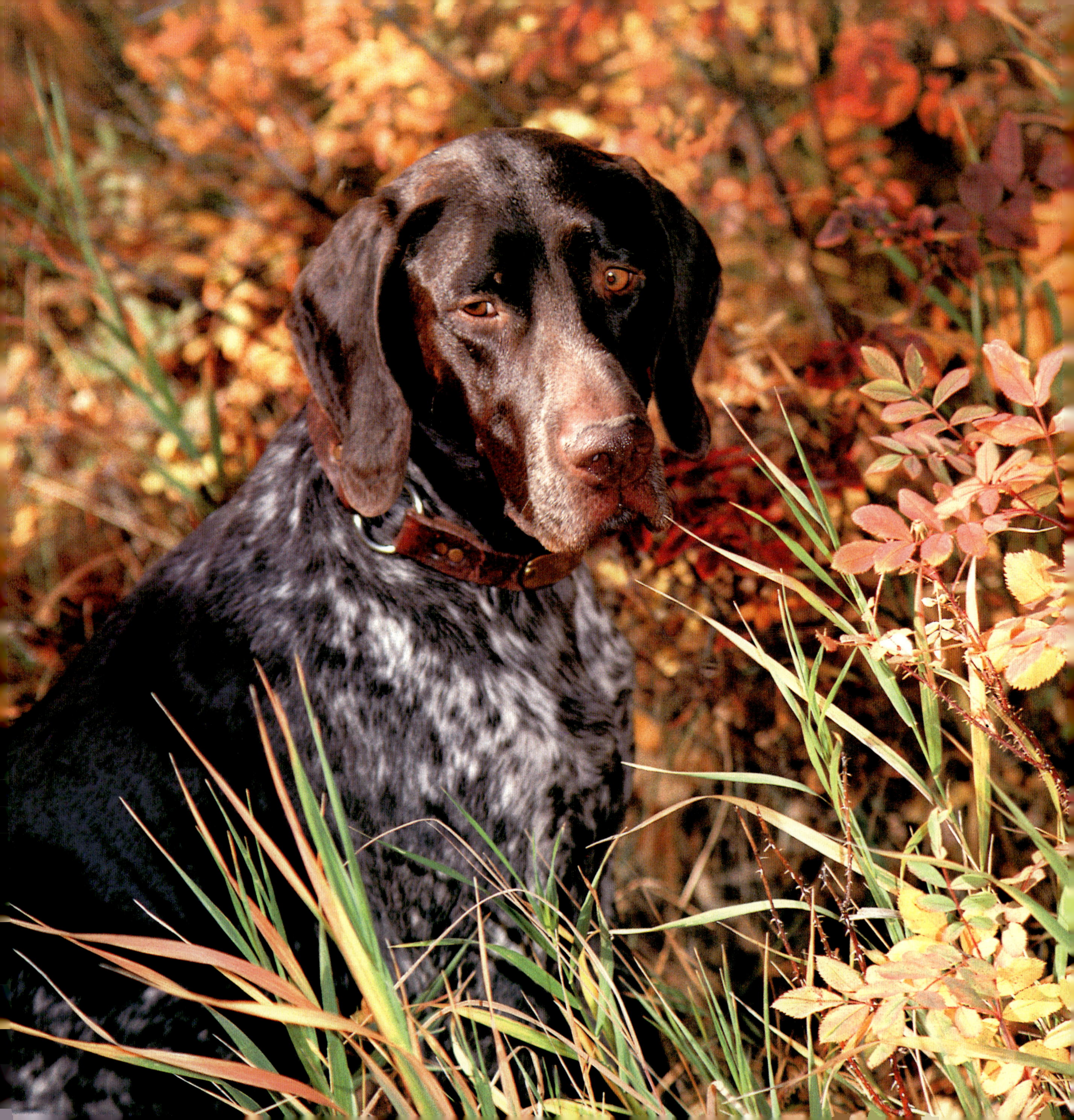

CONTENTS

Introduction 8

Chapter one
The History of the Dog 10

Chapter two
The Refined Dog 36

Chapter three
It's a Dog's Life 62

Chapter four
Canine Care 90

Chapter five
A Gallery of Dogs 100

Further Reading 122

Appendix 124

Index 125

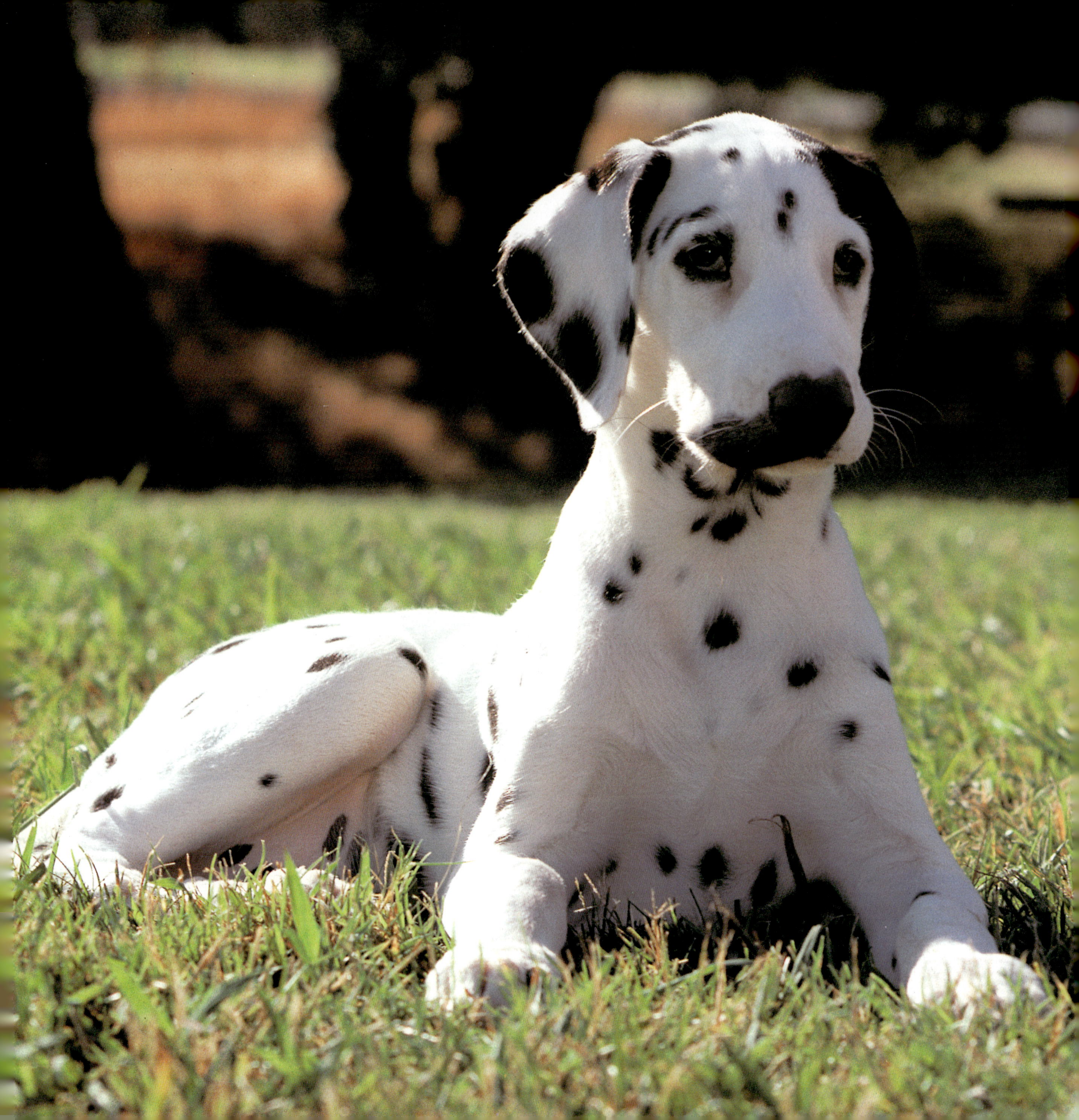

INTRODUCTION

No other animal has shared as much with humanity as *Canis familiaris*, the domestic dog. Indeed, for at least 12,000 years, this creature, but one paw-step away from the wolf, has willingly and happily traded freedom for an uncertain relationship with mankind.

Humanity's relationship with the dog has spanned the gamut of our experience. The dog was a silent, uncelebrated partner at *Homo sapiens'* own beginnings. Later targeted as an object of superstitious scorn, the dog was called "werewolf" or worse. Yet the dog's greatest role has been as partner and beloved companion.

Whether exploited, despised, or pampered, the dog has remained our staunchest companion. Dogs have hunted, gone to war, and been both beaten and rewarded by humans; they have retrieved our game and guarded our flocks; and they have loved us with unconditional fervor.

Why do humans love dogs? There are a variety of reasons—dogs are cute as puppies, and handsome as adults; they depend on us; pedigreed animals are a status symbol. But ultimately, we love dogs because they love us. Our dog loves us in spite of all our flaws and wriggles with delight at the mere sound of our step at the door.

The dog-and-man partnership is a symbiotic relationship that defies rational explanation. To a person, a dog may be a wild creature to be caressed and tamed, a mirror to reflect one's emotions, a sharer of sorrows, a giver of happiness, or a bringer of peace. I don't know why dogs love people; I'm just glad they do.

The Dog Companion is a book for dog lovers everywhere. It's a celebration of canine lore and history, and includes basic guidance for novice and seasoned dog fanciers alike. I hope these pages will touch the heart, lift the spirit, and broaden the reader's understanding of the nature of these marvelous creatures that have chosen to share their lives with us.

The dog can be a gift to the human soul. May we be worthy of such devotion.

• Opposite: Dalmatian puppy.

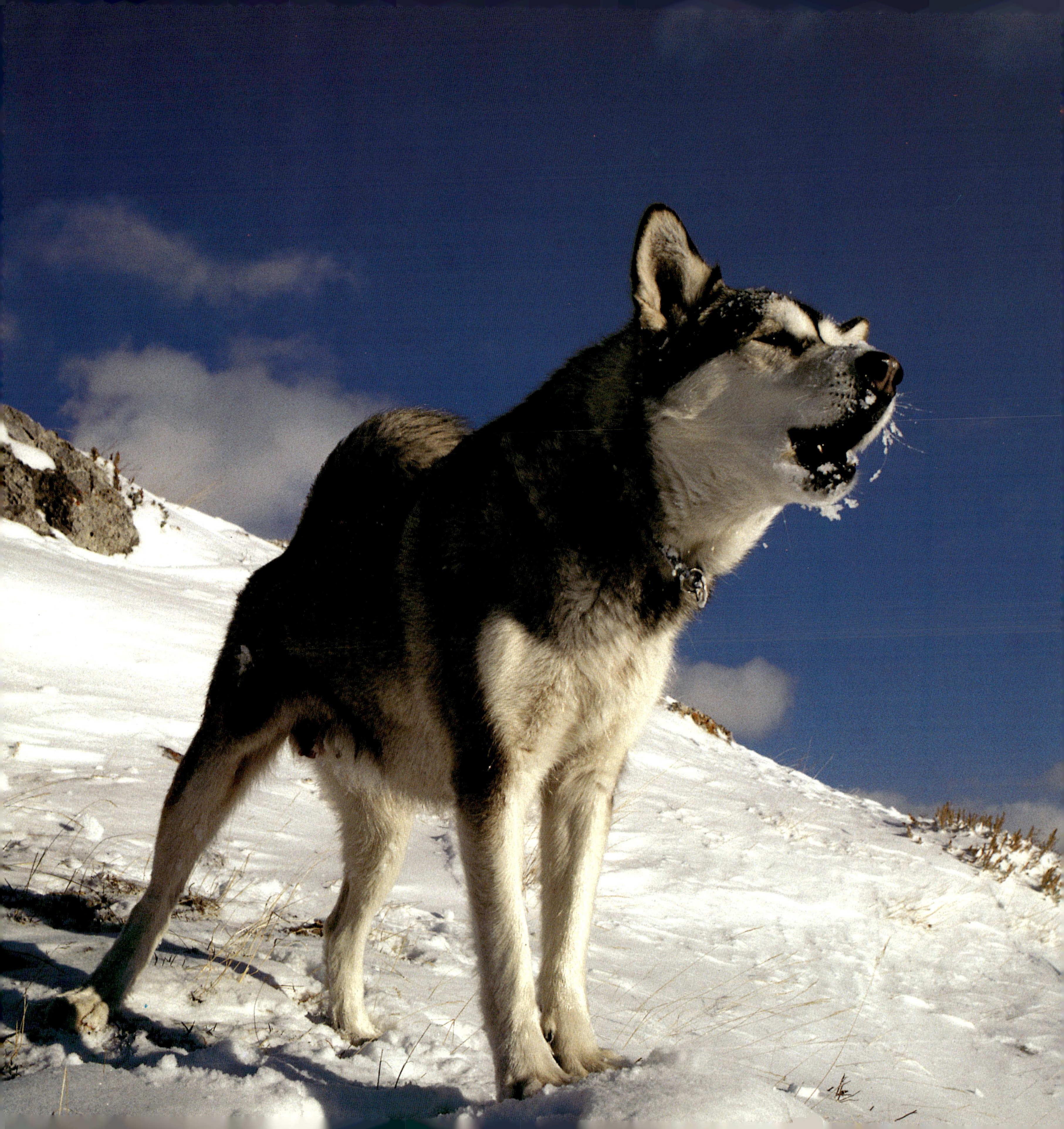

In the beginning, God created man, but seeing him so feeble, He gave him the dog.

—Toussenel

CHAPTER ONE

THE HISTORY OF THE DOG

The pudgy puppy playing tug-of-war with your socks hasn't yet been in the house a full day, and already he's made himself a part of the family. He's left toothmarks on the La-Z-Boy recliner, pooped under the piano bench, and begged and wagged his way into your lap where he now snuggles with a happy little sigh. The longer the dog stays, the harder it will become to imagine life without him.

Dogs as we know them have been part of human lives for many thousands of years. The oldest published radiocarbon date on domestic dog remains are from Iraq and date to 12,000 B.P. But even before humans began domesticating wild canids, dog ancestors shared human history. A fossil site at Zhoukoudian near Beijing, China, shows evidence that early *Homo erectus* and wolves lived in the same environment as early as 500,000 years ago. There is no proof that these wolves were domesticated, however.

• Opposite: Malamute.

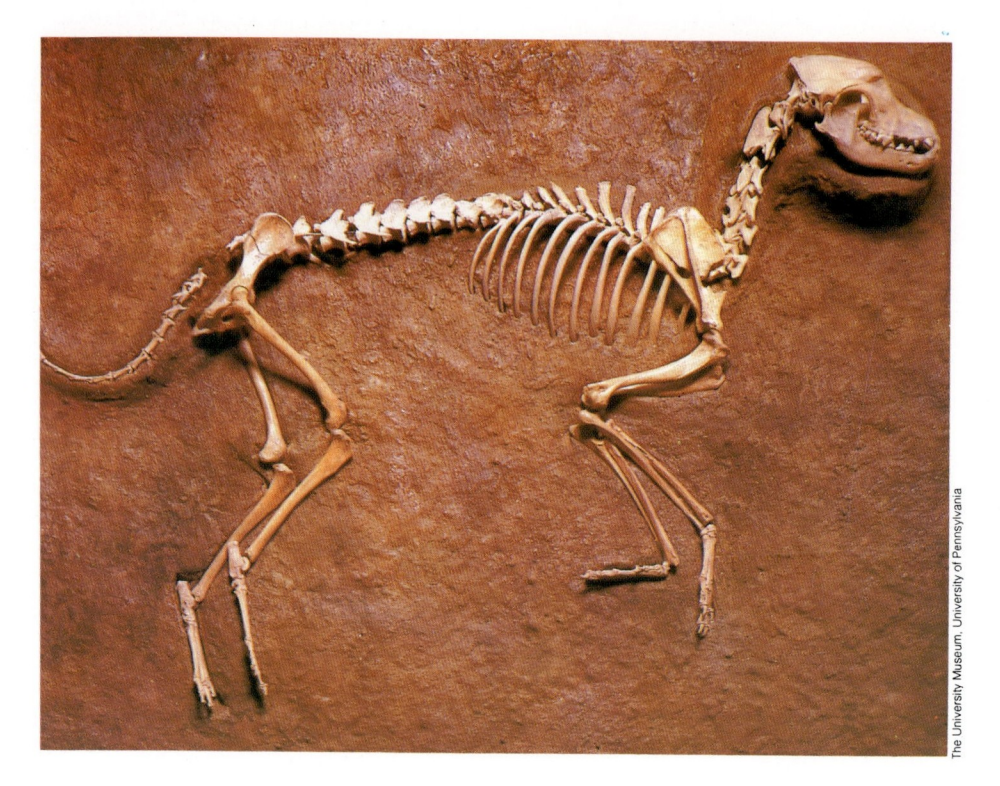

• Above: This canine skeleton dating from 1450–1150 B.C. was found buried adjacent to human remains in a prehistoric cemetery near Hajji Firuz, Iran.

Dogs are carnivorous (meat-eating) mammals, which are classified within the Order Carnivora and Family Canidae. Canids possess large, conical, canine teeth for puncturing and tearing flesh, and elongated bladelike "carnassial" cheek teeth for shearing meat. Modern land carnivores are all classified within the sub-order Fissipeda, which means "Cleft Foot" (having toes, as opposed to carnivores with fin-feet, like seals). Fissipeds appeared about 61 million years ago during the middle Paleocene epoch, and quickly diversified into new types of animals. Some became plant eaters, while others developed into even more accomplished land carnivores.

Miacids were small, shrewlike animals, the largest only about the size of a fox and the smallest about the size of a ferret. Their bodies were long, with relatively short legs, flat feet, and a long extended tail. They probably looked like modern-day pine martins. Miacids were remarkably successful, forest-dwelling carnivores, and fossils showing skull size tell us that they were much smarter than their ancestors. Scientists speculate the Miacids had retractable claws and were arboreal (tree-climbing), much like today's house cats.

This resemblance of a dog ancestor to cats isn't surprising. Carnivores include members of the bear family (Ursidae), the badger family (Mustelidae), the hyena family (Hyaenidae), the civet, genet, and mongoose family (Viverridae), the raccoon family (Procyonidae), the cat family (Felidae), and, of course, the entire dog, fox, and wolf family (Canidae).

Members of the family Miacidae were early carnivores that gave rise to all the modern families of the Order Carnivora at the beginning of the Oligocene epoch, about 40 million years ago. This means that dogs and cats are actually distantly related. Could this have something to do with the supposed ancient enmity between the two species?

Miacids are found at the base of the family tree; they branch into two distinct evolutionary paths: the Aeluroidea or "Catlike Form," and the Canoidea, the "Doglike Form." The Catlike forms (Viverridae, Hyaenidae, and Felidae) have retained the solitary stalk-and-pounce behavior of their Miacid ancestors.

A DOG'S LIFE

The Canoids apparently originated as hunters in the open grasslands. The digitigrade (toe-walking) foot enabled these mammals to run faster over longer distances than many other carnivores. Claws became blunted, and paws were no longer used like hands to capture or manipulate prey (as in cats). Instead, canid jaws developed into the characteristically elongated snout, which is better adapted to capture and hold the victim. Some species (like modern Cape Hunting Dogs and wolves) developed social "pack" hunting, a practice that enabled them to bring down much larger game. With communal hunting came a need for better communication, and sophisticated vocalizations, facial expressions and body scents, coded fur coloring for better distance identification, and the "semaphore" ear-and-tail-movement signals were developed.

The flat-footed bear and the two-walking dog diverged from the rest of the Canoidae in Oligocene times. Although they remain similar in general structure, bears became huge, almost totally herbivorous forest-dwelling animals, while the canids stayed smaller and remained more mobile carnivores.

Mesocyon, the "Half Dog," was a coyote-size animal that lived in the Miocene epoch, some 35 million years ago. The digitigrade foot and leg structure identified it as a forebear of the two-walking, sprinting canines. Mesocyon was long-bodied and short-legged, with shearing carnassial teeth and a massive skull with a short muzzle. It probably looked more like a hyena than a dog. Another Miocene species, *Amphicyon* ("Around Dog") was a gigantic, primarily herbivorous animal that was eventually replaced by the true bears. Today, many dog breeds still resemble, at least superficially, their Ursidae cousins. Some early forms of canidae were exclusively carnivorous, as in the instance of *Hesperocyon*, which is the earliest recognized animal in the direct line of dog evolution. This dog was a small, house cat–size animal that hunted much like a modern fox, with stealth followed by a pounce.

The carnivore *Leptocyon*, possessed a body and dentition that were recognizably foxlike in appearance. This animal appears in the fossil record in the late Oligocene and is in a direct ancestral line leading from the Miocene forms to the more modern *Canis*.

Scientists have never been able to prove with any certainty the direct wild ancestor of the dog. In the nineteenth century, Charles Darwin theorized that crossbreeding the wolf, *Canis lupus*, and the golden jackal, *Canis aureus*, perhaps resulted in the forebears of today's dog. The theory held that certain dog breeds resembled the wolf, while others looked more like jackals.

Other scientists believed there was a separate unknown animal, now long extinct, from which our modern dogs evolved. However, no such "missing dog-link" has ever been found. More recently, both theories have been discredited.

Another theory postulates that modern domestic dogs are descended solely from wolves. Wolves evolved from

• Above: A wooden figurehead (A.D. 1400) probably of the Calusa Indians, found buried in a southwestern Florida swamp, uses exaggerated ears, a characteristically long nose, and sharp teeth to portray the wolf.

THE HISTORY OF THE DOG

- Right: Poodle.

a hyenalike animal, originating in the Western Hemisphere in the Oligocene epoch, and living through the Miocene epoch (about 15 million years ago). The wolf was probably domesticated during the Neolithic age, perhaps earlier. Fossilized bones of a small wolf (*Canis lupus variabilis*) have been found in a number of early-to-late Pleistocene locales in China along with *Homo erectus* remains, although there is no evidence that the wolf was domesticated at all. It is generally accepted that the basic ancestral animal was this or a similar subspecies of the wolf, and that China is one of the most likely areas of the first domestication. Today, most experts agree that the wolf alone is the direct ancestor of our domestic dog.

Canine Cousins

The science of taxonomy, which classifies and defines links between different kinds of living things, is one of categories and divisions. Animals belong in the kingdom Animalia, in which they are further categorized into phylum, class, order, and family. Dogs are designated as the family Canidae. Animals grouped within the family are divided according to structural similarities; this category is known as the genus. Finally, animals within a genus are categorized by species, and some even further into subspecies. The species is the only taxonomic category that has biological meaning, and may be tested through breeding experiments. Truly separate species cannot interbreed and produce fertile offspring. The subspecies, or variety, category is often evoked to name or describe hybrids.

About 10 million years ago, the family Canidae developed into the huge variety of animals that consists of the fourteen living genera we recognize today. Jackals, coyotes, wolves, and domestic dogs all share the same genus. All domestic dogs, no matter what their size or shape, belong to the family Canidae, genus Canis *species* familiaris—*our own "Familiar Dog."*

WILD VERSUS TAME

The Cocker Spaniel puppy proudly carries a shoe into the family room, pauses, and sheepishly wags its tail at your exclamation of surprise. As you try to retrieve the sneaker, you play a brief game of tug-of-war with the fiercely growling ball of fluff, before he willingly relinquishes his prize, then yaps and bounces, begging for another game. Take a moment to consider: What exactly does that rambunctious, endearing puppy have in common with its wild cousins in other parts of the world? How are they alike; what are their differences?

Canines all over the world are remarkably similar. Like all placental mammals, they have live births and suckle their young. Most canids have a gestation period of about sixty-three days, and their young are born with closed eyes and ears, and in large litters. Most canids are

Coyotes, extending their ranges into eastern Canada, are interbreeding with Timber Wolves. This new breed, midway in size between the two species, has a thick coat well suited to the cold, wet climates of the East. The new animal now makes its home in parts of New Hampshire and Maine, some probably interbreeding with domestic dogs, further clouding what type of animal it truly is.

primarily meat eaters. The physical family likeness includes a long, typically doglike muzzle; large, mobile, erect ears; an expressive tail; and a muscular, agile body.

Most canids live in a small family group consisting of the male and female parents and first-year pups. Only wolves, the Dhole, and Cape Hunting Dogs are known to live in extended family communes. The hunting technique of wolves, Dholes, and Cape Hunting Dogs calls for speed and tirelessness, in which they simply wear down their prey in marathons of endurance, rather than using the stalk-and-ambush technique of cats. The sheepdog tirelessly driving his flock reflects the mastery of the wolf that shadows the caribou and skillfully cuts out the weakest prey from the herd; the terrier ferrets out and catches rats with the dexterity of the fox; and the dog that raids the household garbage scavenges as naturally as the jackal. It's easy to see the many resemblances between the wild and the tame.

Canids are physiologically so similar that all may potentially interbreed and produce fertile young. Dog-and-wolf crosses are not only possible, but are quite common and often encouraged; offspring have characteristics of both parents. Dogs and jackals also can be easily crossed. There have even been hybrid animals produced from successful crossbreedings of wolf, dog, and jackal.

Skeletal structure in wild canid species is very uniform, the most striking difference being size-related. This difference is primarily due to function. Obviously, in order for the northern wolf to capture the large prey of the tundra, it must be much bigger than the small Kit Fox, which subsists primarily on mice and rodents. Environment also dictates the distinctive fur coats among canids. The Arctic Fox wears white in winter to blend into a snowy background, then changes to slate gray to match the environment of warmer seasons.

Wild canids bark only when defending their den to draw attention and lead predators away. But their pups bark all the time, and so do most adult domestic dogs.

• Above: Cape Hunting Dog.

THE HISTORY OF THE DOG

15

Domestic dogs have been bred by humans into the wide range of shapes, colors, and sizes familiar to us today. This artificial selection of characteristics reflects the many purposes to which the domestic canine has been pressed. It hardly seems possible that the short-legged, long-bodied Dachshund and the huge Neapolitan Mastiff could really belong to the same genus, let alone the same species.

Unfortunately, there is not space to discuss all of the many interesting varieties of the wild canids. Due to the great number, the following represents the most unusual or significant of the wild species.

WILD DOGS

The term "wild dog" generally refers to a canid that hunts prey its own size or larger. All wild dogs rely on endurance to overcome their prey, and are superb runners and trotters. Wild dogs have long, heavy jaws designed for crushing bones, and wide, short, bearlike ears located on the sides of their heads. Wild dogs live in packs or tribes made up of several generations. Cape Hunting Dogs and Dholes are two examples of modern wild dogs.

Cape Hunting Dog

The Cape Hunting Dog, also called Hyena Dog for its resemblance to that creature, is probably the most ancient of the wild dogs. Cape Hunting Dogs reach about 3.5 feet (1m) in length, have erect, bearlike ears, and live in the grasslands and open savannas south of the Sahara. Named *Lycaon pictus,* or "Spotted Wolf," the Cape Hunting Dog is the only wild canid to have irregular spotty markings of white, brown, and black. This unique coloration isn't camouflage, but instead serves as a means of visual identification over long distances.

The Cape Hunting Dog is the only wild dog to have four toes on both fore and hind feet, rather than the typical five on the front and four on the back. It also has a functional collarbone, where most canids have only a remnant of cartilage.

A DOG'S LIFE

The retention of infantile behavioral characteristics, such as barking, is apparent in almost all domestic dogs. This is a distinct difference between wild and domesticated canids. Such puppyish appearance or behavior in adults is called "neoteny."

Most domesticated dogs are "lop-eared," with their ears hanging limply over their cheeks. Even straight-eared breeds like the German Shepherd retain floppy ears through much of puppyhood. All wild canids have erect ears from shortly after birth on.

The curved (or sickle) tail is another sign of neoteny. Wild canid puppies carry their tails spiked straight up, but wild adults always hold their tails at a downward angle when not using them to communicate. Compare this with the tails of nearly all domestic adult dogs, which curve up even when the dog is at rest.

The Cape Hunting Dog is a sight hunter, much like Greyhound breeds of domestic dogs. It lives and hunts in packs of up to sixty animals, roaming over wide areas to prey on zebra, warthog, gazelle, and wildebeest. Cape Hunting Dogs share food by regurgitating partly digested meat to feed nursing females, the ill, and the young when the pack returns from hunting.

It is said that Assyrians and Egyptians used Cape Hunting Dogs from the fifth to the twelfth dynasty to course antelope. When replaced by a dog resembling the present-day Fox Terrier, Cape Hunting Dogs were abandoned and returned to the wild.

• Center: A Cape Hunting Dog feeds another pack member by regurgitation.

THE HISTORY OF THE DOG

• Above: Dingo.

These canids are known for their comical fascination with puppies. Upon return from a hunt, adults often stumble over each other in their eagerness to play with and feed the babies. Adults of both sexes often adopt orphaned pups to raise.

Dhole

The short-haired Dhole *Cuon alpinus* (Mountain Dog) is found on the Indian Subcontinent and in Southeast Asia. The Dhole resembles the fox, and typically has fox-red fur with a black-tipped tail. The Dhole communicates by whistles, cries, yaps, howls, barks, and whimpers. Primarily a forest dweller, the Dhole is a fearless, efficient hunter that will even attack tigers.

Dingo

The Dingo *Canis dingo* is the only wild canid of Australia. This barkless dog reaches about 4 feet (1.2m) in length, and is a silent hunter with strong jaws capable of breaking the spine of a kangaroo.

Some scientists believe Dingos descended from the Phu Quoc dogs of eastern Asia, or were carried to Australia by ancestors of the Aborigines. During the Pleistocene, when massive glaciers held much of the world's water frozen, lowered sea levels permitted early humans to cross the narrows between the Asiatic mainland and Australia. Australia was the Dingos' paradise. Within a few thousand years, Dingos spread across Australia and displaced the marsupial "wolves," which are now extinct in all but a few remote areas of Tasmania.

The Basenji of North Africa not only looks very much like the Dingo, it is probably also descended from a similar canid ancestor. The Basenji is one of the oldest purebred dogs in existence, and appears in Egyptian art that dates back 5,000 years. Like wild canids, adult Basenji dogs don't bark, unless taught by other domestic breeds.

Bush Dog

The Bush Dog *Speothos venaticus* looks like a squat, short-legged dog with a bear's head. All canids cock hindlegs and urinate to scent-mark territory, but female Bush Dogs actually back up and "hand-stand" to mark turf. The Bush Dog is a forest dweller that lives in dense undergrowth along rivers. It is an excellent swimmer, and will go into the river after prey.

Several domestic breeds share the Bush Dog's fondness for water. In particular, retrievers like nothing better than swimming, and will dive enthusiastically into a pond, lake, river, or stream at the least provocation.

A DOG'S LIFE

Raccoon Dog

The Raccoon Dog, also called the Japanese Fox *Nyctereutes procyonoides*, is found in China, Japan, and the far eastern reaches of Russia. Its thick, fleecy coat is colored and marked like that of the familiar raccoon. It lives in temperate and subtropical forests, along rivers or in marshy areas, subsisting on a diet of fish, frogs, rodents, and acorns. The Raccoon Dog, unlike any other dog, is able to become semi-dormant during the winter months.

Terrier breeds were developed originally for eradicating vermin, and many continue to find great joy in hunting and catching rodents and other small game, just like the Raccoon Dog. As for hibernating, I personally know of several dogs that do a fair imitation.

Fox

"Fox" is the common name for all small wild canids, many outside the genus *Vulpes*. Foxes are smaller than wild dogs; none stand higher than the human knee, and many are as small as house cats. The fox hunts alone, and mainly at night, depending mostly on its senses of smell and hearing rather than on sight. In many ways, foxes are more like cats than dogs; they use cunning and stealth instead of speed in hunting. Moreover, the pupils of a fox's eyes close to slits just like those of a cat.

The fox's luxurious fur is highly prized by furriers the world over. As demand for its pelts grew, the fox became famous for its wiliness in evading hunters and trappers, and was often celebrated for its cleverness and cunning in fable and folklore. The fox's weakness for blueberries, cherries, apples, grapes, sweet corn, squashes, and melons often tempt it to steal from field and vine.

The fox ranges from scorching deserts to the frozen Arctic. Some species, like the North American Gray Fox, *Urocyon cinereoargenteus*, prefer the woods and often climb trees to nest in hollows far above ground. The Fennec, *Fennecus zerda*, is strictly a desert animal that lives in excavations beneath sand dunes. Its enormous ears act both as radar and as radiators to help rid the body of excessive heat.

In some cultures, it is believed that charms made in the likeness of the fox will bring success in business, because the fox's cunning affects the wearer.

• Above: Red Fox.

THE HISTORY OF THE DOG

19

Above: Black-backed Jackal.

A god of ancient Egypt, Anubis, was conductor of the souls of the dead. Anubis was the cleansing god, the guardian of the gates of the underworld. Today, historians argue over whether Anubis was the jackal or the domestic dog. Both, it seems, had the same fondness for bodies of the dead.

Jackal

Jackals *(Canis aureus)* are relatively small canids that reach a maximum body length of about 2.5 feet (75cm). Although jackals may prey on small animals, they mostly live off the leavings of others. Jackals are primarily nocturnal and rarely form packs; they usually live in pairs or in small families, much like the fox. Some bold jackals venture into villages and steal poultry, earning the enmity of humans.

Maned Wolf

The rare Maned Wolf (*Chrysocyon brachyurus*) may reach a body length in excess of 4 feet (1.2m), and is the largest South American canid. Its name comes from the luxuriant crest of long hair that extends from the nape of the neck to the shoulders. It has a distinctly foxy appearance, both in the shape of the face and fur coloring, but its long, narrow legs give the Maned Wolf a conspicuously odd look. The natives call it "fox-on-stilts," and indeed, it hunts by the fox's stalk-and-pounce method and buries excess food for its future use.

Coyote

The Coyote *(Canis latrans)* looks like a small wolf. Coyotes were originally confined to the prairies of North America, where they preyed on prairie dog, deer, and pronghorn. When human hunters eliminated its prey, the Coyote became a semi-scavenger like the jackal. The Coyote now eats mostly small animals and carrion, and also fruit, tubers, and plants when it is very hungry. Coyotes usually live alone or in pairs, and both parents help rear the young. Coyotes, much like wolves, use eerie howling to communicate and feces and urine to mark territory.

The Navaho Indians of North America have many stories and legends in which the Coyote is a recurring figure. Coyote is a master trickster from whom not even the gods are safe. During the creation when the night sky was made, instead of carefully placing the stars, Coyote haphazardly flung them in one mass and created the Milky Way.

A DOG'S LIFE

Ornaments made in the likeness of the wolf keep bad luck from entering the house. It is considered good luck to have a wolf cross your path.

Wolf

At last we come to the wolf *(Canis lupus)*, the largest member of the Canidae. There are thirty-two subspecies of the present-day wolf recorded worldwide, and some may reach 31 inches (77.5cm) at the shoulders, 4.5 feet (1.5m) in length (not including the tail), and weigh as much as 175 pounds (79kg).

Wolves are extremely adaptable and can live in both grasslands and open woods. Although wolves are powerful enough to take large musk oxen and caribou, they prefer the smaller deer, wild sheep, and goats. Wolves are intelligent hunters and whenever possible choose prey that is more easily brought down—younger, older, and/or weaker animals. Wolves may run alongside their prey, slashing and tearing at it until the victim is weakened enough to be killed; one wolf may grab the prey by the nose and hang on, while others close in for the kill. Sometimes wolves drive an animal in relays until it falls from exhaustion, or they may herd an unwary victim into the jaws of waiting associates.

Wolves are true pack animals, living and hunting in extended family groups consisting of father, mother, and pups from both the current and previous years. In lean years, several families may band together and form packs of a dozen members or more. Wolves establish their territory by scent-marking and howling, and a rigid social order is maintained within the pack. Wolves normally mate for life, and both parents care for pups. Often, the death of one of a "married" pair of wolves may be followed by the death (from sadness?) of the other, even if the remaining partner is healthy.

Wolves are the domestic dog's closest wild relative. Scientists believe that the smallest, the Asiatic Wolf *(Canis lupus pallipes)*, was the first forebear. Even today, many of the northern sled-dog breeds retain a distinctive wolfish appearance. When humans first domesticated dogs, they invited the wildness of the wolf into the parlor.

Just listen to the fervent yapping of the diminutive Chihuahua or the baleful baying of the Bloodhound; watch the Greyhound's graceful sprint and the Pomeranian's mincing step; feel the Bulldog's wet snuffling kiss; thrill to the uncanny howls of the Malamute. No matter the wrapping, it's obvious that beneath the fur lies the heart and soul of the wolf.

Humans have long watched and envied the hunting prowess of the wolf. The ancient Greeks considered Apollo a wolf-god, and the Arcadians worshiped Zeus as a wolf-god. Norsemen sought to capture the wolf's skill through the magic of naming. Beowulf ("War Wolf") may be one of the most famous examples, and even the ships of the Norsemen were called "sea wolves."

Similarities between the social behavior of wolves and humans have resulted in the many stories of children being raised by wolves. One of the most famous of these myths celebrates Romulus and Remus, brothers who later founded Rome.

• Below: Timber Wolf.

THE HISTORY OF THE DOG

CANID CLASSIFICATION

GENUS *CANIS*
- Side-striped Jackal, *Canis adustus*
- Golden Jackal, *Canis aureus*
- Black-backed Jackal, *Canis mesomelas*
- Simenian Jackal, *Canis simensis*
- Dingo, *Canis dingo*
- Domestic Dog, *Canis familiaris*
- Coyote, *Canis latrans*
- Wolf, *Canis lupus*
- Red Wolf, *Canis niger*

GENUS *VULPES*
- Bengali Fox, *Vulpes bengalensis*
- Southwest Asian or Banford's Fox, *Vulpes canus*
- Cape Silver Fox, *Vulpes chama*
- Gray Fox, *Vulpes cinereoargentatus*
- Corsac Fox, *Vulpes corsac*
- Tibetan Sand Fox, *Vulpes ferrilatus*
- Indian Desert Fox, *Vulpes leucopus*
- Pale Fox, *Vulpes pallida*
- Sand Fox, *Vulpes ruppelli*
- Swift or Kit Fox, *Vulpes velox*
- Red Fox, *Vulpes vulpes*

GENUS *DUSICYON* (SOUTH AMERICAN CANIDS)
- Zorro, *Dusicyon culpaeolus*
- Culpeo Fox, *Dusicyon culpaeus*
- Zorro, *Dusicyon fulvipes*
- Pampas Fox, *Dusicyon griseus*
- Zorro, *Dusicyon gymnocercus*
- Inca Fox, *Dusicyon inca*
- Zorro, *Dusicyon sechurae*
- Zorro, *Dusicyon vetulus*

GENUS *ALOPEX*
- Arctic Fox, *Alopex lagopus*

GENUS *ATELOCYNUS*
- Zorro, *Atelocynus microtus*

GENUS *CERDOCYON*
- Crab-eating Fox, *Cerdocyon thous*

GENUS *CHRYSOCYON*
- Maned Wolf, *Chrysocyon brachyurus*

GENUS *CUON*
- Dhole, *Cuon alpinus*

GENUS *FENNECUS*
- Fennec, *Fennecus zerda*

GENUS *LYCAON*
- Cape Hunting Dog, *Lycaon pictus*

GENUS *NYCTEREUTES*
- Raccoon Dog, *Nyctereutes procyonoides*

GENUS *OTOCYON*
- Bat-eared Fox, *Otocyon megalotis*

GENUS *SPEOTHOS*
- Bush Dog, *Speothos venaticus*

• Right: Artic Fox.

Primal human and wolf societies were very similar: both were composed of relatively small units, were capable of hunting larger game either in the open or wooded areas, and utilized team effort. In addition, human hunter-gatherers and wolf packs shared food with weaker non-hunting members of the group, like wolf pups or human infants. Very probably, humans also noticed that the howling of the wolves paralleled their own vocal communication.

FROM WOLF TO WHELP

How did early man and the wolf get together? About 100,000 years ago, humans and wolves were probably rarely in direct competition for food. In the northern regions of Eurasia, humans concentrated on hunting woolly mammoth and rhinoceros, while wolves preferred smaller prey. Wolves didn't become important to people until the decline and extinction of the big, slow-moving game. Then humans were forced to turn to much fleeter, smaller prey, and became direct rivals of the wolves.

It's hard to ascertain exactly how our early ancestors hunted, but more than likely they were as aggressive as their wolf competitors. It's reasonable to assume the wolf was domesticated not by design, but for mutual benefit. Humans admired the wolf's ability to track by scent, while the wolf enjoyed the leftovers of the human hunt.

Archeological evidence shows that Stone Age humans often killed entire herds of animals, stampeding them with fire until they became mired in mud, or were driven off cliffs. Only a few animals were actually eaten, while the rest were left to rot. Early humans were surely in awe of the wolf's ability to determine weak members of the herd and "cut" them out for the kill; such ability was useful to humans. During the Mesolithic period (about 20,000 to 10,000 years ago) hunters seem to have selected good herders from the wolves following them.

Wolf pups in the wild participate in wolf society; when raised with humans, they transfer this affection to men and women. The first wolf cub adopted into human society would likely have assumed that it was a hairy human—or that its companions were hairless wolves—and enthusiastically treated the humans as members of its pack.

Ancient cultures recognized and admired the hunting prowess of wolves, which figured prominently in their legends and myths. Such myths are closely associated with wolf-cults, members of which adopted the wolf as a totem and imitated wolf behavior. The ancient Celts believed the horned nature-god Cernunnos was often accompanied by a wolf. The wolf was also companion to Odin, chief god of the Norse pantheon, and the Norse underworld was inhabited by a god known as Fenris-wolf. Fenris-wolf symbolized chaos and the everlasting ice fields that would one day return to engulf the world. Perhaps this story derives from some primal memory of man roaming the ice floes in the company of wolves.

• Below: Werewolf scares were common in Europe, as this fourteenth-century print shows. Opposite: Samoyed.

Werewolf lore (lycanthropy) reflects man's fear of the wolf's powers—and perhaps, of his own capacity for savagery. Werewolf scares occurred quite frequently during medieval times, and werewolf hangings were common; the afflicted human supposedly reverted to wolf form at death. Wolf cults prospered for some time during the Christianization of Europe.

By the early sixteenth century (during Henry VII's reign), wolves were extinct in England; they were no longer in existence in Scotland by the eighteenth century, but according to legend, may have lingered until 1848; they disappeared from Ireland in 1821. The last Japanese wolf was reported in 1904. Today in North America, only relic populations survive.

The "polar" or "spitz" dog breeds are among the earliest of the modern dogs. They seem closest to their wolf cousins and originally shared the ranges of nomadic people living within the Arctic Circle. Canis familiaris palustris, or the Peat Dog, appeared during the Neolithic Age (6000 or 5000 B.C.) and managed to spread across Europe. The Peat Dog was sized midway between the jackal and fox, and possessed a tapering muzzle, a wide, deep chest, and slight legs. The Peat Dog would probably look similar to a modern-day Samoyed or spitz. Today's polar dogs include Huskies, Malamutes, Norwegian Elkhounds, and others.

The Dingo of Australia and the Pariah Dog of southern Asia and northern Africa are very similar ancient dog types. Both are short-haired, medium-size dogs with curled tails; their coats come in a variety of colors.

Gazehounds and sight-hunting dogs were probably bred from Dingo-Pariah stock selected for speed in crossing open country. Gazehounds vary in coat color and length, but are almost uniformly long-legged, narrow-headed, and lightly built. The Saluki of Asia Minor may be the most ancient existing purebred dog today. Other gazehounds include the Borzoi, Collie, Whippet, and Afghan Hound. From the early polar, gazehound, and Dingo/Pariah dog types sprang the immense varieties of breeds we know today.

A DOG'S LIFE

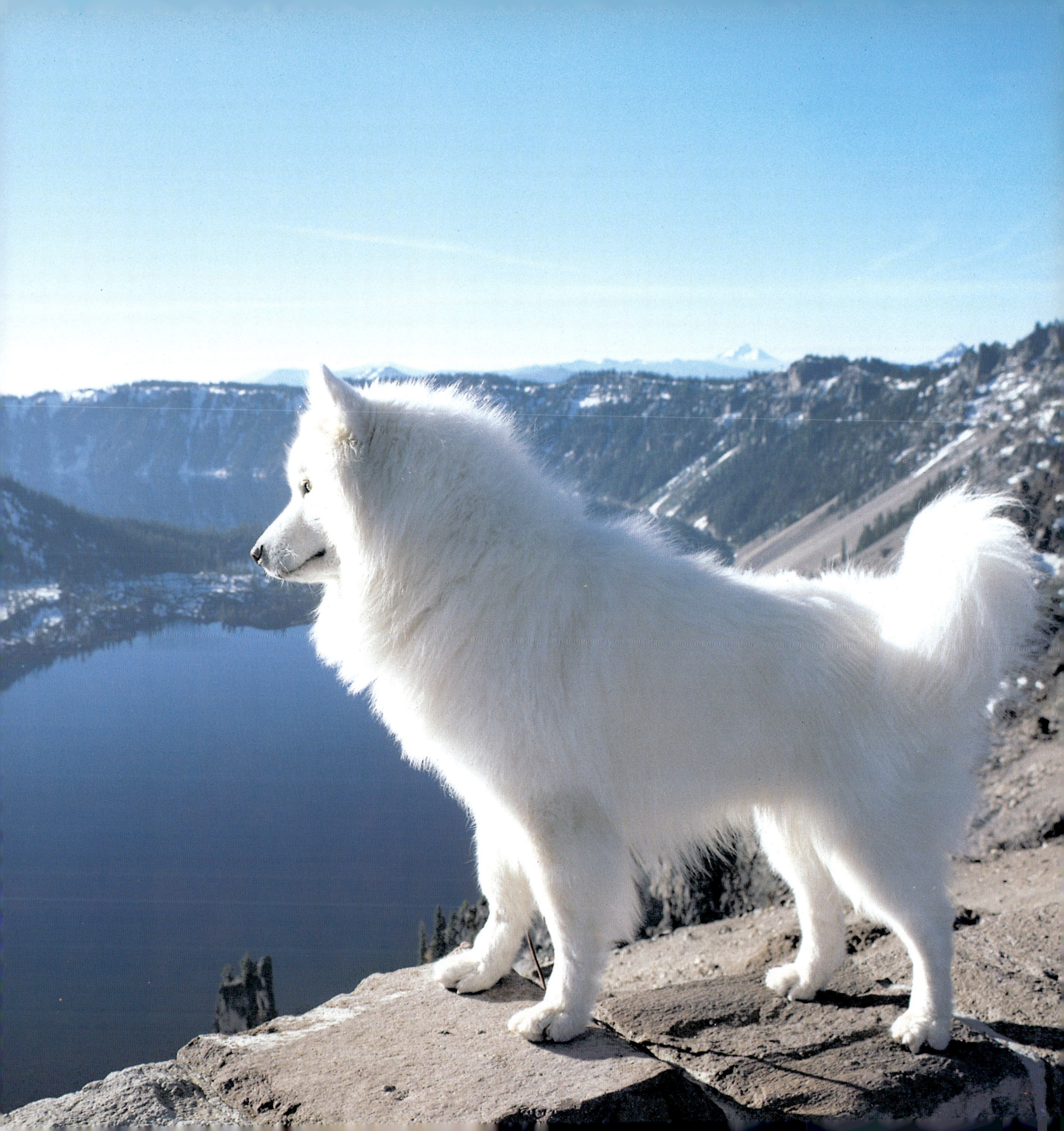

When the dog was created, it licked the hand of God and God stroked its head, saying, 'What do you want, dog?' It replied, 'My Lord, I want to stay with you, in heaven, on a mat in front of the gate...'

—Marie Noel

The first noticeable changes in tamed wolves reflecting domesticity are a foreshortening of the muzzle, crowding of the tooth rows, and a comparative overall reduction in tooth size. The teeth of modern dogs haven't changed very much from those of their ancestors 15 million years ago; based upon a single tooth, it's hard to tell if a canid fossil belonged to an early dog or came instead from a local wild species of wolf. Some of the earliest "short-faced" wolves that crossed the border between wildness and domestication were animals larger than, but otherwise much resembling, today's modern Eskimo dogs.

Exactly when did the wolf shed its wild ways and become a dog? That question continues to baffle experts and will probably never be satisfactorily resolved.

Whatever the answer, it matters little to the dogs of today, or to the humans who love them. Suffice it to say that dogs and people have been enriching each others' lives for eons. Ancient peoples considered wolves "four-legged humans," and surely our present-day dogs can be considered no less. Dog and human are in many ways two sides of the same coin, each so a much part of the other's life that a separate existence is no longer conceivable.

HISTORY OF THE DOG

People have long bred dogs for a variety of uses. But where did the first dogs appear? Domesticated dogs probably originated in Mesopotamia; from there, they gradually spread throughout Asia and Europe. But a nearly parallel, simultaneous development of the human/dog partnership is found in almost every civilization of the world.

The Americas

In North America, the earliest dogs were found at Jaguar Cave, Idaho, carbon-dated 9500 to 8400 B.C. In 1921, two dog mummies of Basket Maker Dogs were discovered at White Dog Cave in Arizona. These date from around the birth of Christ. Both were found with fur-robe-wrapped human mummies.

Two types of dogs were common to ancient Mexico. The first served as beloved companions, and were very similar to the Chihuahua we know today. The other was

• Above: An 1875 Cheyenne Indian drawing. Plains Indians often used dogs to carry supplies.

A DOG'S LIFE
26

medium size with brown markings, and looked something like the early Egyptian and Greek dogs (similar to modern Dalmatians).

The Aztec civilization of Old Mexico occupied an ecosystem lacking large mammals suitable for food. Aztecs instead ate ducks, turkeys, and a wide assortment of domestic dogs like the famous bald Xoloitzcuintli, or Mexican Hairless.

European dogs were brought to the New World by Christopher Columbus during his second voyage. Those twenty dogs originally served as food tasters. They were also used to hunt game, and were themselves eaten when game was scarce. The Native American people greatly feared these kinds of "devouring dogs," which were instrumental in the victory of the Conquistadors.

The *moneria infernal* (infernal hunt) offered pleasures for the Spanish conquerors, who considered the natives little more than animals. Dogs were used to punish and terrorize. In organized spectacles, they were pitted against one or several unarmed Native Americans. This supposedly trained the young dogs to attack and devour.

Egypt

Dogs have been bred in the Middle East since at least 4000 B.C. Egyptian murals show many types of Greyhounds; these dogs were very successful in desert countries where the hot, still air made scenting difficult but allowed excellent visibility. Some dogs had upright bat-ears like the modern Ibizan Hound, while others had small drop-ears with the feathering of the Saluki.

Dogs were often depicted in Egyptian art. Hunting scenes in the tomb of Tiy, wife of Amenhotep III (1417–1379 B.C.) show various domestic types ranging from the Greyhound to the spitz. A wooden casket in the Cairo museum shows Pharaoh Tutankhamen (1370–1352 B.C.) standing upright in his chariot shooting arrows at enemy soldiers while his cream-colored, spike-collared Mastiff dogs attack them.

Later pharaohs preferred cats for hunting in the marshes, but continued to use the Greyhound for hunting antelope. A Dalmatian-type dog eventually took the place of the Greyhound. The Pharaoh Hound was probably used along with cats to protect grain from rodents. Pictures in tombs at Beni Hasan, Egypt, show it to have changed little in 2,000 years.

Although Egyptians worshipped cats, they adored dogs as well. About 4240 B.C. the upper Egyptian culture worshipped Set, a Greyhound figure with a forked tail. Dogs were never considered subordinates by the Egyptians—they were hunting dogs, war dogs, even temple dogs, but always equals. Killing a dog was punishable by death. Only slaves or children acted as shepherds of livestock, an occupation considered too lowly for the dog. After death, the dog was embalmed and its remains placed in a sarcophagus; the dog's human family mourned its passing with weeping and by shaving their entire bodies.

[The Greyhound is] one of the rare creatures that knows how to walk gracefully.

—*Solomon, c. 1000 B.C.*

• Left: This pottery jug from the late fourth century B.C. was found in Apulia, South Italy. It depicts Paris, son of the King of Troy, with his faithful sheepdog. Paris later abducted the legendary beauty Helen of Troy, and thus began the Trojan War.

THE HISTORY OF THE DOG

27

Ancient Greece and Rome

The dog of Greece was both a warrior/hunter and a guardian of the flock and the house. Early Assyrian wall paintings (c. 625 B.C.) show large, heavy Mastiff–like dogs with wrinkled heads and curled tails apparently used for hunting wolves and lions. These dogs were treasured and bred by Greeks who called them Molossians, and the Romans gave the group its modern name of Mastiff (from *mansuetus,* or "tame," referring to their use as family guard dogs). Alexander the Great (356–323 B.C.) was so fond of a Mastiff–type dog given to him by the king of Albania that he had a whole town built in its memory. By the time of Christ, Mastiffs were common in much of the civilized world.

Overall, the Greeks weren't terribly concerned with dogs. Plutarch says dogs were not tolerated in Athens, and a Roman priest who stroked a dog had to purify himself before he could take part in any sacrifices. Statues of the physician Hippocrates (460–377 B.C.) often depicted him with a snake beneath his feet and a dog at his side, symbolizing the common fatal afflictions of the time: poison and rabies.

The citadel of Corinth was guarded by fifty dogs. One night, the dogs defended Corinth from a surprise attack, and all were killed but one. The lone survivor ran back to the fortress to raise the alarm and managed to save the city. In gratitude, a marble monument to the memory of the brave dogs was erected. The surviving dog, named Soter, was given a pension for life and a solid silver collar inscribed, "To Soter, defender and savior of Corinth, placed under the protection of his friends."

- Above: Depiction of a dog on a granite stele at the Ramses II outdoor museum in Memphis, Egypt.

In Rome, owning dogs was a privilege of the leisure class, and it was fashionable to keep dogs in the house. Less-monied folk made do with geese as household guardians. Dogs were also used for communications. These dogs were made to swallow metal tubes containing secret messages; upon delivery, the dogs were sacrificed to recover the message.

The Romans' war-trained "devouring dogs" were starved for several days before combat to make them more ferocious. Roman war Mastiffs often wore their own armor, with leather-mounted knives fixed to collars, backs, and sides to damage the enemy's legs and horses. Some dogs were fitted with torches, which frightened the horses and disrupted enemy cavalry charges. Mastiffs were also employed to attack and frighten elephants that were used to carry archers in classical times.

The Persian kings also used ferocious dogs for war. Cyrus the Great released four towns in Babylon from taxes, for which exemption they were required to breed and train combat Mastiffs for his army.

Mastiffs continued to be used as war animals into the sixteenth century; Henry VIII of England beat Charles V of Germany by sending 500 starving dogs into battle.

A DOG'S LIFE

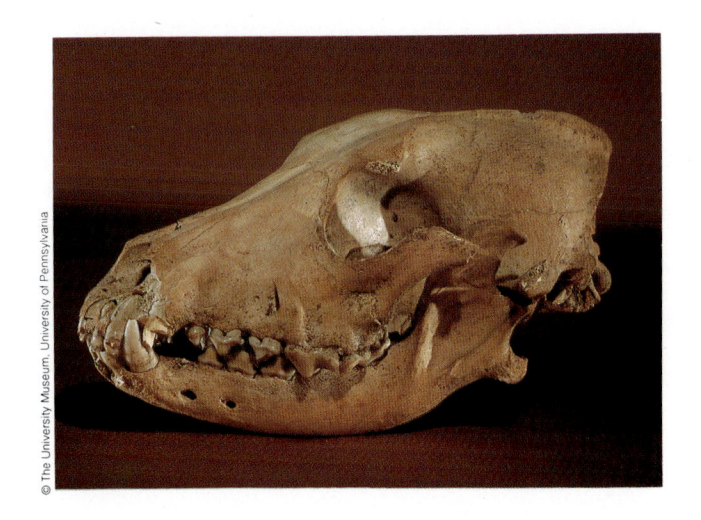

Persia

In early Persia, the dog was treasured for its work as shepherd of the flocks and protector of humans. It was considered a crime to kill dogs and a duty to cherish them, according to the decree of Ormuzd, the Son of Fire. Ancient Persians called their great and wise men Khan (the Dog), which symbolized gentleness and wisdom.

A custom of early Persians required delaying the burial of close relatives of their seers until the dead body was ripped apart by wild beasts. The great Roman statesman Cicero (106–43 B.C.) wrote in Book One of *The Tusculan* that poor people in Persia used the village's stray dogs to do so, while richer folk used their own household dogs.

The ancestors of today's Pariah Dogs were probably shepherds forsaken when herding was abandoned. Today in India, Pariah Dogs commonly devour garbage and corpses, and are often offered water because of their good work as cleansers of the streets.

Modern Moslems regard the dog as unclean. Islamic legend holds a dog guilty of devouring the body of Mohammed, and tradition has demanded that dogs be hanged in the streets as punishment for the crime.

Eastern Asia

About 3468 B.C., Fo-Hi of China encouraged the breeding of tiny "Sleeve Dogs." The Chinese in A.D. 100 were breeding "Pai Dogs," which were short-legged, short-mouthed dogs that "belonged under the table."

The Shih Tzu (Son of Lion) has been bred since A.D. 624. China also produced the Pug, introduced to Europe by traders of The Dutch East India Company in the seventeenth century. But the most ancient dwarf dog, called "Little Lion-Dog" or "Butterfly-Lion" is the Pekingese, dating from at least 3,000 years ago.

Dog meat was often part of royal banquets, served alongside roast beef, pork, and ram. Chow Chows represent selective breeding of polar-type dogs, and were used both for food and as temple guards.

The early Pekingese were so dwarfed and twisted that stunted jaws made it impossible for them to eat normal food. As a result, the babies of slave girls were killed, and the dogs were fed by nursing from the childless women.

Among the pantheon of early Japan was Omisto, the god of suicide. Omisto had the body of a man with head of a dog, and rode a charger with seven heads. Omisto promised eternal joy to any man who killed himself in Omisto's honor.

• Top: The skull of a Saluki dog dated 3500 B.C. found in northern Mesopotamia (Tepe Gawra, Iraq). Left: A brick made in 2100 B.C. found in Ur, Iraq, stamped with the builder's inscription—and dog footprints.

THE HISTORY OF THE DOG

The Celts who settled in Gaul (France) in the fifth century B.C. followed a Gallic religion in which their god Smertulus was the "devouring dog," a symbol of destruction and death.

Europe: The Dog in Disfavor

The Middle Ages were centuries of turmoil for Europeans, but more so for their dogs. Countless dogs followed soldiers and were abandoned all along their travels. Ownerless dogs wandered the cities, living on garbage, and banded together to scavenge the countryside. Those that survived quickly reverted to a semi-wild state and copied their ancestors' proclivity for digging up and feeding upon corpses.

Only the wealthy minority could afford to keep dogs. The rest of the populace saw only the terrifying packs of scavenging wild dogs, which filled them with superstitious fear. Many peasants readily believed the legends of fantastical creatures. Devil dogs, werewolves, dog-

In 1685 in Germany, a dead burgomaster was said to have ravaged the countryside as a werewolf. The unpopular King John of England was also reputed to have become a werewolf after he died. In those days, anyone with physical peculiarities, such as extreme hairiness or eyebrows that grew across their brow, was suspect.

headed dragons, and other hideous canine creatures leered from church architecture as gargoyles and flourished in the imagination of the people. The words "dog" and "cur" became curses. The Catholic Church's Second Council of Macon (A.D. 585) forbade priests from having dogs guard their houses "as much because of the noise and salacious behavior of these animals, as because of the poison [possibly rabies] which is transmitted in their bite."

Inadvertently, the cat saved the dog from continued vilification; the cat was guilty of having been made a god in Egypt. When the church turned its attention to eradicating "feline evil," the dog was reinstated as companion and faithful servant.

- Right: In many European countries, dogs have been used as work animals. Strict laws are enforced to prevent abuse or neglect.

A DOG'S LIFE
30

William the Conqueror (1028–1087) demanded every dog not belonging to him should have three toes cut off to slow its speed. King Francis I of France (1494–1547) decreed, "All dogs belonging to peasant or farmer must wear, attached to their necks, a heavy block of wood, the weight and bulkiness of which will stem their ardor, whenever they move away from their homes. If despite this precaution they take to hunting on royal land they will be punished...by hamstringing...." And Henry III of England (1551–1589) issued an edict in 1578 barring commoners from hunting, upon pain of death.

THE CELEBRATED DOG

In England and Europe, wealthy nobles maintained packs of hounds for stag, wolf, or boar hunting, and imposed laws and penalties for the protection of their dogs. Monasteries began breeding dogs and trying to create new specialized breeds for the nobility. The first was the Saint Hubert Hound, produced by the monks of the Abbey of Saint-Hubert at Mouzon in the Ardennes in the eighth century. Given as a gift to the king of France, this valuable Bloodhound became quite common in less than twenty-five years. From these first Bloodhounds were derived a vast array of scent hounds, from giant to miniature.

Nobles often purchased dogs at inflated prices, trying to improve their lines. During his travels, King Louis IX of France (1226–1270) brought back the grey dogs (gazehounds) with which he had hunted gazelle in the Holy Land. Crossbreeding these dogs with existing breeds created a number of new specialty dogs: large Wolfhounds and Mastiffs for hunting bear or wild boar, smaller dogs to flush birds, and setters to drive game into nets. Soon, the right to hunt became reserved as a privilege of class. Hunting was no longer a means of obtaining food; it had become a sport.

Hunting dogs were prized and pampered. Eventually this "harmless" pastime of princes and kings began to bother the Church. Noblemen presented themselves for Mass with their hounds at their feet. When reproached for bringing dogs into the church, the hunters refused to be separated from their furry companions, and heard Mass outside, with all the church doors open. Indeed, Charles IX of France (1550–1574) was so fond of "Courte," a white water Retriever called a Griffon, that he allowed her to eat from his own plate. When she died, he had a pair of gloves made from her hide to keep her near him.

Small dogs were no less prized. Terriers were originally used with ferrets to kill rats. The ferrets were released down burrows to "flush" rats to the surface, where the dogs would kill them. This sport was known as "ratting." A fifteenth-century cartoon even shows terriers chasing rats in a hospital ward. A good ratting terrier killed hundreds of rodents a day; according to *The Guinness Book of Records*, a Bull Terrier named Jenny Lind once killed 500 rats in 1.5 hours.

By the end of the Middle Ages, the dog's position had improved from a source of fear and hostility to that of privileged hunter. With the advent of the Renaissance, the dog became a friend as well.

• Above: Emperor Charles V and his faithful canine companion as depicted in a portrait by Titian.

Louis XI (1423–1483) was so fond of his dogs that he ordered a gold collar studded with rubies for his favorite greyhound, "Cherami."

THE HISTORY OF THE DOG

The word "terrier" is derived from the Latin terra *or "earth"; a terrier will "go to earth" and follow prey even into the burrow if necessary.*

• Right: Jack Russell Terriers.

A DOG'S LIFE

THE RENAISSANCE DOG

In this time of prosperity and plenty in Europe, dogs were kept by the wealthy, the working class, and even farmers. Dogs of all shapes and sizes were everywhere; Mastiffs rode beside wealthy Italian citizens, and at court and in castles all over the continent, the ladies pampered tiny, miniature versions of hounds and bushy dogs.

The sport of "baiting" became popular. From the thirteenth century on, dogs in England were cruelly pitted against each other or other animals for the pleasure of human observers. Bulldogs and Bull Terriers were originally produced for cattle management at the butchers, and their aggressiveness and tenacity made them well suited for the bloody sport of baiting.

Not all dogs had it so rough, though. Some were performers or workers that turned spits in kitchens; others filled more traditional roles as sheepdogs. By the eighteenth century, pampered lap dogs became the rage; Pugs, Papillons, and Maltese had their fur cropped and crimped to match their mistress' hairstyle of the day. But hunting dogs remained the pampered pooch of choice. They ate with their masters and often slept in their bedrooms.

The French Revolution and the fall of the monarchy (1792) brought an end to privilege of rank in France, and hunting finally was permitted for commoners. Pedigreed dogs bred for pack hunting with horses became obsolete, and the Napoleonic wars and social unrest ended the lines of many breeds. English breeders concentrated on perfecting a gun-dog, and the setter was developed. From this dog was derived the pointer, shown for the first time in France in 1860.

RECENT HISTORY

By 1851, for the first time in England's history, more than half the population lived in urban areas. The expanding middle classes and their rising social aspirations caused an unprecedented demand for luxury. Owning a dog was the epitome of refinement.

In England, the Royal Society for the Prevention of Cruelty to Animals (RSPCA) was formed in 1837, with the Australian branch opening in 1871. The American SPCA was founded in 1866, the American Humane Association in 1877, and the Toronto Humane Society

• Above: Ben Marshall (1767–1835), *Huntsman on Foot and Hounds.*

THE HISTORY OF THE DOG

In 1576, France's annual budget for royal dogs reached 100,000 gold crowns. Henry III (1551–1589) was very open in his love of dogs and would often appear for the most serious occasions wearing a ribbon-trimmed basket hung from his neck in which rested several little dogs (Papillons).

in 1887. Veterinary medicine made great strides during those years. Dogs owe a debt of gratitude to Louis Pasteur (1870–1914), who finally perfected a vaccine against the dreaded rabies. In 1920, a diabetic dog was saved by insulin for the first time at the University of Toronto. Once anesthetics were perfected, surgeries to correct all sorts of ailments were made available, and veterinary medicine began to flourish.

Interest in breeding new varieties and refining old breeds persisted well into the nineteenth century. The great hunting dogs and pack hounds had already been listed in "stud books" of ancestry, and with the first dog show in 1859 in England came interest in establishing the lines of other breeds. The Kennel Club in Britain was formed in 1873, shortly followed by similar organizations in other countries.

Today, breeders continue to perfect and redefine all kinds of dog. Breeding clubs have standardized many breeds, and keep meticulous records of bloodlines. There are more than 150 different dog breeds officially recognized around the world.

The new order of working dogs aren't necessarily of specific breeds. Guide and signal dogs, bomb- and drug-sniffing dogs, and search-and-rescue dogs may be a variety of purebreds, or even mutts. You name the task, a dog will do it.

It is the generic "pet dog" that has outdistanced all others in popularity. Today, there are millions of pet dogs all over the world. Whether pampered purebreds or cherished mutts, their work as "companions" has brought them closer to humans than at any time in the past. Truly the dog is *Canis familiaris*—faithful dog.

- Right: Dogs, like humans, need to exercise to stay healthy.

A DOG'S LIFE

THE HISTORY OF THE DOG

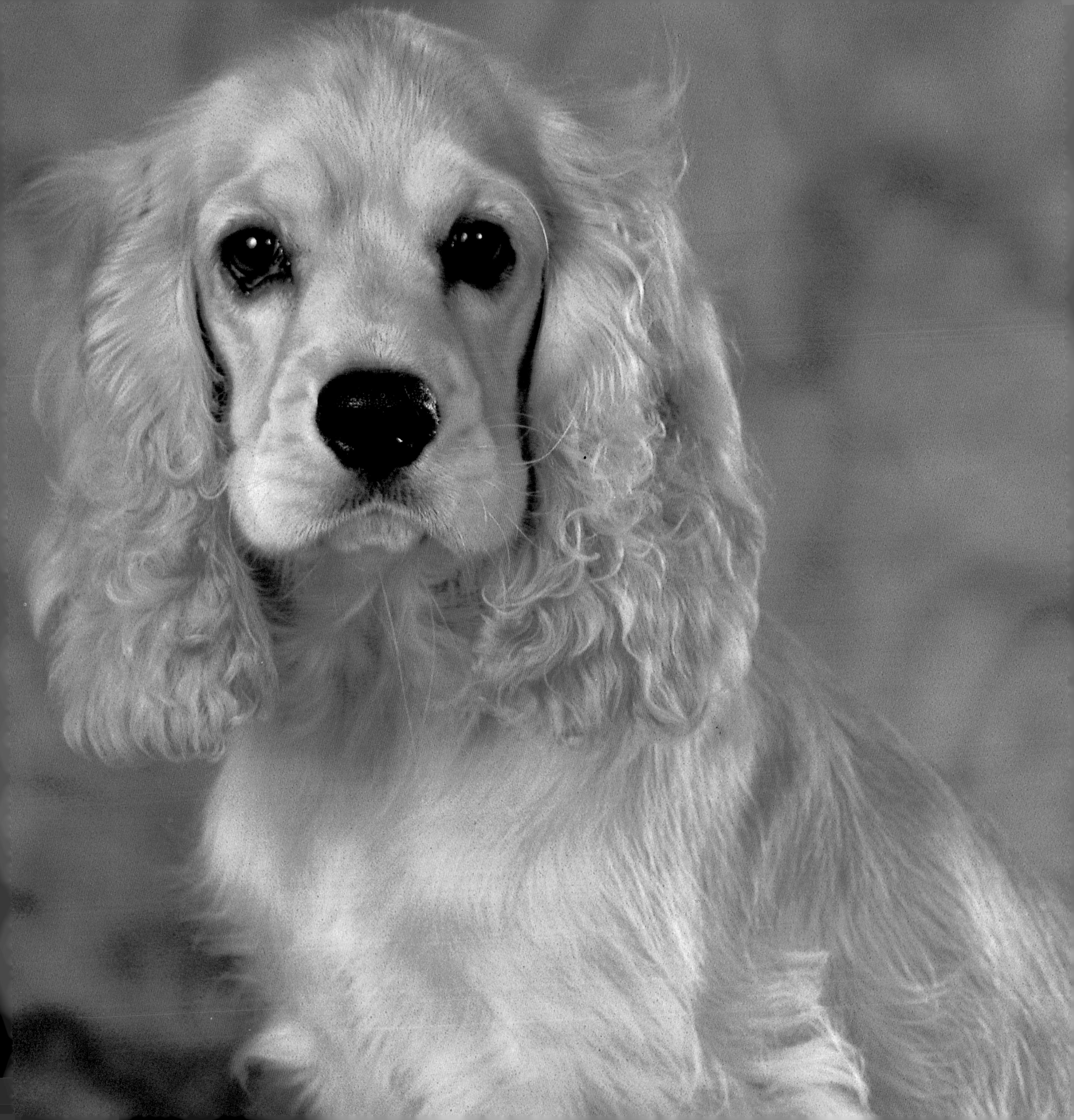

Outside of a dog, a book is man's best friend. Inside a dog, it's too dark to read.

—*Groucho Marx*

CHAPTER TWO

THE REFINED DOG

CANINE LITERATURE

The dog has inspired artists for centuries. Writers have celebrated the dog's love, devotion, and steadfast loyalty perhaps more than that of any other animal. Many authors express a profound passion for the dog, and it is quite obvious that the feeling is mutual.

The classical poet Homer, who lived in Ancient Greece about the ninth century B.C., was probably the first to introduce the dog in literature. In the *Odyssey*, Homer tells the moving tale of Argus, the faithful, beloved dog of Ulysses. Abandoned, starving, and scorned by his master's friends, Argus pathetically dragged himself about the streets until Ulysses finally returned to Ithaca after twenty years. Argus died of happiness at finding his master once more.

The Greek philosopher Aristotle (384–322 B.C.) was another early author who wrote fondly of the dog. He

• Opposite: Cocker Spaniel.

THE REFINED DOG
37

praised the courage of the Laconian Mastiffs and listed the most useful breeds of the time. The Roman poet Virgil (70–19 B.C.) wrote of the great debt owed to the swift Bloodhounds of Sparta. Both the scholar Varro of Rome (116–27 B.C.) and later, the poet Ovid (43 B.C. to A.D. 16) described the best dogs to own, and where to find them.

The Roman scholar Pliny the Elder (A.D. 23–79) held forth on the affections of the dog, and even wrote a natural history that included the dog. Arrien (second century) wrote a work regarded as an authority for centuries on the 1,000 secrets of hunting with dogs. The Greek fabulist Aesop attributed to the dog all the virtues and vices of a human. His fable of the dog sleeping in the ox's hay is probably the source of the term "dog in the manger," referring to a selfish person who jealously guards something from others even though it may be useless to himself.

Literature is filled with authors that either adore and celebrate the dog, or ridicule and despise it. The saying *Qui me amat, amat et canem meum* ("Love me, love my dog") is credited to St. Bernard of Clairvaux, a French clergyman who lived during the twelfth century. The English poet Geoffrey Chaucer (1342–1400) was the first to say, "It is nought good a slepyng hound to wake."

Writers of the Middle Ages often made the lowly dog the butt of pointed political and moral barbs. Jean La Fontaine (1621–1695), a French poet, seemed to take particular pleasure in demeaning the dog. Although he acknowledged the dog to be a symbol of duty and devotion, he believed the dog was also a stupid and greedy animal, overflowing with shortcomings. In "The Wolf and the Dog," La Fontaine writes contemptuously of the "willing slavishness" of the dog compared with the freedom of a wolf, which would rather starve than wear a collar. In his fable "The Dog and His Master's Dinner," the dog spinelessly shares his master's meal with three other dogs rather than defend it in the face of sure defeat: "An excess of devotion is not worth fighting for."

Popular opinion during the Middle Ages held the dog in contempt. Rabies presented a very real threat, and masses of abandoned dogs roaming and scavenging for their existence did little to better a seedy reputation. The very word "dog" came to mean a worthless or inferior person; the expression "dog-eat-dog" probably referred to the sorry strays that were marked by a ruthless, competitive self-interest, which was the only quality that allowed them to survive. To "dog it" meant to be a shirker; to "go to the dogs" was to fall into ruin; a "dog's chance" was almost no chance at all; and to lead a "dog's life" was to have a miserable, dismal existence.

Even literature had its own doggy pejorative. "Doggerel" was a type of comic or burlesque verse that was considered trivial and inferior.

• Above: *Cave canem*, an Italian mosaic dating from the first century A.D.

A DOG'S LIFE
38

My profits have gone to the dogs,
My trade has been such a deceiver,
I fear that my aim
Is a mere losing game,
Unless I can find a Retriever.

Thomas Hood (1799–1845),
Dog-grel Verses

The Renaissance saw the revival of interest in art and science, and an ability to appreciate and utilize the dog as never before. In the twelfth century, an English Franciscan monk named Bartholomew Ganville had published a book on animal medicine which became widely read only now. The renewed interest in the dog led to the publication of a number of such books, including George Turberville's treatise *The Selection, Hygiene and Illnesses of the Dog.*

For ages there had probably been people who preferred the company of dogs to their own kind, but at this time authors actually admitted the fact. The French author Paul Scarron (1610–1660) acknowledged his dog in print: "To Guillemette, my very honest and amusing dog. Although you are only an animal, I prefer nevertheless to dedicate this book to you, rather than to some great satrap whose sleep I would thereby be troubling."

Still, some men of science divorced themselves from the emotional attachment to dogs. The philosopher René Descartes (1596–1650) considered the dog nothing but a piece of machinery, lacking feelings or emotions; his colleague Blaise Pascal (1623–1662) shared Descartes' scorn for the dog. But not everyone agreed with these great men. The Marquise de Sévigné (1626–1696) responded, "Machines which love, which prefer one person to another, machines which are jealous...come now! Descartes never thought to make us believe that!" The English poet William Blake (1757–1827) even compared the treatment a man gave his dog to the country's social health: "A dog starved at his master's gate/ Predicts the ruin of the state."

As the dog's popularity increased, so did its defenders. According to the French essayist Michel de Montaigne (1533–1592), "The friendship of a dog is without a doubt more intense and more constant than that of a man."

The French fabulist Florian (1755–1794), like Aesop and La Fontaine before him, used fables featuring animals to prove points, but he treated the dog with more sympathy. In "La Brebis et le Chien" ("The Sheep and the Dog"), the sheep tries to induce the dog to join him in a revolt against the cruelties of man. But the dog wisely refuses, noting that it's always better "to submit to evil rather than to do evil."

• Left: Mixed breed.

THE REFINED DOG

During the Romanticism of the eighteenth century, it became quite acceptable to express one's feelings for pets. By the nineteenth century, the dog was perceived as "Faithful Fido," staunch defender and companion of man. Writers celebrated the dog in romantic, sentimental poetry. In 1844, Elizabeth Barrett Browning (1806–1861) wrote a tender tribute to her dog, "Flush":

...Therefore to this dog will I,
Tenderly not scornfully,
Render praise and favor

Alphonse de Lamartine (1790–1869) was a French poet who kept and loved dogs. "The more I see of the representatives of the people, the more I admire my dogs," he said. He wrote in "Le chien du solitaire" ("The Lonely Man's Dog"):

Never have I kicked you in scorn,
Never with a brutal word saddened your tender love,
My heart has never repulsed your touching caress
But always...Ah, always in you I honor
The ineffable goodness of your Master and mine.

Other renowned poets to embrace the dog in their work include the American Robert Frost (1874–1963), Hartley Coleridge (1796–1849), and Scot Robert Burns (1759–1796). Even American songwriter Stephen Foster (1826–1864) honored the dog in his song "Old Dog Tray." Later, the English poet A.A. Milne (1882–1956) and the American Odgen Nash (1902–1971) poked gentle fun at the dog in humorous verse.

Epitaphs for beloved dogs were a favorite literary form of many writers. Sir Walter Scott (1771–1832) built a marble mausoleum at his house at Abbotsford, Scotland to the memory of Maida, a Scottish Deerhound. It bore the inscription *Sit tibi terra levis* ("May the earth lie lightly on you"). Scott said of the dog, "Recollect that the Almighty, who gave the dog to be companion of our pleasure and our toils, hath invested him a nature noble and incapable of deceit."

A DOG'S LIFE

Rousseau's favorite dog, Turk, inspired the following epitaph: "My poor Turk was only a dog, but he loved me. He was sensitive, disinterested.... As you yourself said to me, how many so-called friends were not worth this one!" The English poet Lord Byron (1788–1824) owed his life to a Newfoundland dog named Boatswain, which found him when he was lost and injured as a child. In 1808, he erected a monument to Boatswain with the following inscription: "Near this spot are deposited the remains of one who possessed beauty without vanity, strength without insolence, courage without ferocity, and all the virtues of Man, without his vices. This praise, which would be unmeaning flattery if inscribed over human ashes, is but a just tribute to the memory of Boatswain, a dog."

As the nineteenth century progressed, the perception of dogs became less clichéd, and a variety of noble, wicked, and commonplace dogs were represented in literature. The French writer Victor Hugo (1802–1885) adored dogs and wrote about the dogs that shared his life. "The dog is virtue which unable to make itself man, became beast..." he once noted. Apparently, dogs loved him as well. A Poodle he gave to a diplomat living in Moscow ran away, and within a few months found its way back to Paris and was discovered scratching at Hugo's door.

The English novelist Charles Dickens (1812–1870) celebrated the dog in countless books and stories, describing Bouncer the Pomeranian, Don the Newfoundland, and Sultan the hunting dog in *My Father as I Recall Him*. The French author and artist Jean Cocteau (1889–1963) wrote and illustrated the book *Un drole de menage* (*A Strange Family*). In it, a couple named Lord Sun and Lady Moon were too busy to properly raise their children, who became cruel, stupid, and wicked as a result. The pet dog was then entrusted with raising the children, and it taught them to be good, patient, and obedient.

The English author Rudyard Kipling (1865–1936) was a dog lover, who said of his Cocker Spaniel, "He is my most sincere admirer; he loves me though he has never read my work!" Toward the end of Kipling's life he wrote the story "Thy Servant a Dog," and in his poem "The Power of the Dog," Kipling warns of the pain that is sure to follow if one loves a dog too much—for the dog will die, and its owner will be left bereft: "Brothers and Sisters, I bid you beware/ Of giving your heart to a dog to tear."

- Top: Newfoundland puppy. Center: Sled dogs figure prominently in Jack London stories.

THE REFINED DOG

A dog's best friend is his illiteracy.

— Ogden Nash (1902–1971)

• Below: This painting by artist Oliver Kemp brings to mind Jack London's novel *The Call of the Wild*.

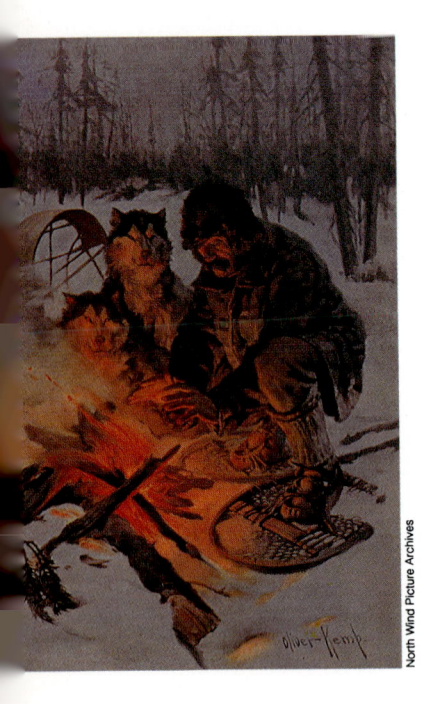

Dogs have been featured frequently in American literature as well, from their roles as hunting dogs in William Faulkner's novels to background characters in stories of the frontier. Dogs set the scene in Mark Twain's *Huckleberry Finn*, in which the "loafers" of the village delight in their cruelty to stray dogs. Twain seemed touched by the plight of the dog. Even his short stories dealt with the sorry reality of the dog's life. In "A Dog's Tale," a brave little dog is rewarded for her heroism and courage by having her puppy selfishly sacrificed to prove a meaningless point, whereupon she dies of sorrow.

Stephen Crane's short story "A Dark-Brown Dog" gives another evocative example of a dog's life. "Down in the mystic, hidden fields of his little dog-soul bloomed flowers of love and fidelity and perfect faith." Sadly, such perfect love was not reciprocated by Crane's story-family.

Zane Grey (1872–1939), whose novels about the American West remain very popular, enjoyed hunting and the companionship of dogs. Of the more than forty dogs to have appeared in his stories, many were victims of the unthinking cruelty of men who consider dogs a mere tool. In real life, Grey loved and kept many dogs; two favorites were an Airedale and a Paiute Shepherd. The Paiute was even mentioned in the novel *Stranger from the Tonto*. The story of *Don*, a tale about a brave hound that hunted lions,

If you pick up a starving dog and make him prosperous, he will not bite you. This is the principal difference between a dog and a man.

— Mark Twain (1835–1910)

When I get to heaven, first thing I'll do, Grab my horn, and I'll blow for Old Blue. Saying, 'Come on, Blue, finally got here too.'

— From "Old Blue," an American folk song

was based on fact; however, although the Don of the story never came back, the real-life Don did return from his adventures. Hunting dogs have been not only sources of pride for their masters, but also well-loved companions.

Jack London (1876–1916) has stirred the emotions of dog lovers for generations with his stories of the sled dogs of the icy North. One of his best-known novels is *The Call of the Wild*. The story is told by a St. Bernard mix named Buck, who is kidnapped and sold as a sled dog during the Alaskan gold rush. Buck's adventures bring him near death, on to a great love of one man, and eventually to his destiny as the leader of his own pack of wolves.

James Thurber (1894–1961) devoted himself to the more humorous aspects of the dog/human relationship. His hilarious story "The Dog That Bit People," from *My Life and Times*, tells of an Airedale named Muggs who bit friend and foe alike. The only thing Muggs feared was a thunderstorm, so Thurber's mother rigged a "thunder machine" from sheet metal that she shook to make Muggs come inside the house. In an introduction to *The Fireside Book of Dog Stories*, Thurber summed up his feelings about dogs: "The dog has got more fun out of Man than Man has got out of the dog, for the clearly demonstrable reason that Man is the more laughable of the two animals."

A DOG'S LIFE

● Left: The Disney movie *Old Yeller* tells the tale of a good dog gone bad—from loving companion to rabid renegade.

Countless other authors have immortalized the dog, including O. Henry, Don Marquis, Booth Tarkington, and Arthur C. Clarke. Dogs have appeared in all genres, from stories of the past and the plausible to those of horror and the supernatural, as well as uplifting tales set in the future. Lester del Rey's short story "The Faithful" questions the fate of dogs bereft of their masters after humanity has destroyed itself. The incredible dog in the more recent Dean Koontz novel *Watchers* is a product of genetic engineering and amplified canine intelligence. A chilling tale is told by Ray Bradbury in his short story "The Emissary"; Stephen King preys on the fears of the past with his tale of a dog gone mad in the thriller *Cujo*, and his predecessor Fred Gipson evoked similar gooseflesh in the classic *Old Yeller*. Eric Knight's famous story of the loyalty of a Collie in *Lassie Come-Home* continues to enrapture dog lovers.

Today, the dog is celebrated in literature as never before. Countless books, stories, poems, and even magazines are devoted solely to the glorification of the dog. Those who love the dog know the honor is a fitting one; for is it not the dog alone above all others who is called "Man's Best Friend?"

...The one absolutely unselfish friend that a man can have in this selfish world, the one that never deserts him, and the one that never proves ungrateful or treacherous, is his dog...

— *George Graham Vest,*
"Tribute to a Dog," 1870

THE REFINED DOG

ART OF THE DOG

Our ongoing love affair with dogs was first immortalized in cave drawings. Some of the earliest dog-related treasures were the ancient amulets of the primitive wolf cults, but it wasn't until the advent of classical art in Greece and Rome that the dog began to appear in art with any frequency. By that time, vases were decorated with hunting and family scenes; mythical dog-gods and demons figured in murals on tomb walls; even everyday utensils and formal jewelry featured the dog. Massive bronze and stone bas-reliefs and delicate mosaics depicted dogs of war and the hunt, as well as the cherished pet.

The dogs of the Far East, with their massive bodies, Bulldog heads and endearing snub-nose faces, were preserved by sculptors who crafted the ancient Chinese terra-cotta dogs. The famous Korean Dogs of Fo guarded temple doors until about 550 B.C.

During the Middle Ages in Europe, the dog became a popular model, but the open contempt religious authorities had for dogs kept artists wary: any visual indication that the dog had intelligence or might have feelings was carefully omitted to avoid offending the Church. Dogs didn't appear in early Christian paintings, but canine statues stood as silent stone guardians of many tombs, and doglike features often showed up on menacing gargoyles. The most daring artist showed dogs with aggressive or stupid expressions.

- Above: Govert Flinck (1615–1660), *A Child Holding a Dog.*

A DOG'S LIFE

When the dog's popularity returned, artists' interpretations became more realistic. By the fifteenth century, dogs finally began appearing in religious art, but hunting scenes like Jean Fouquet's *Death at Vincennes* remained the most popular treatment. The German artist Albrecht Dürer's (1471–1528) engraving *Saint Eustace* is also typical of the symbolic art of the time. Many other artists included the dog in their work, and Antonio Pisano, known as Pisanello (1395–1455), and Leonardo da Vinci (1452–1579) both made numerous sketches and studies of the dog.

At the beginning of the fifteenth century, Greyhounds and Mastiffs were often featured in portraits of the nobility. Titian's (1488–1576) *Charles V* and Anthony Van Dyck's (1599–1641) *The Family of King Charles I* are classic examples. Peter Paul Rubens (1577–1640) and Diego Velázquez (1599–1660) also portrayed the dog in their works.

The depiction of dogs in portraits often offered a subtle commentary on the character of the human subject. If the subject was a bully, his dog might be shown chewing on a bone; if he was a kind, just ruler, a docile, obedient dog would lay at his feet.

Soon, smaller dogs started to appear in art. François Clouet (1510–1572) was the first to document the Papillon in his paintings; Paolo Caliari (called Veronese, 1528–1588) painted the Papillon more than any other dog. During the seventeenth and eighteenth centuries, the Dwarf Spaniel of the aristocracy became more noticeable than the hunting dogs of the past. Jean-Honoré Fragonard (1732–1806) put Papillon-Spaniels in almost all his paintings, and Thomas Gainsborough (1727–1788) showed for the first time the large, white Pom of "Mrs. Robinson."

As the dog became a familiar figure in art, even the common dog began to catch the attention of artists. Pierre Mignard (1612–1695) shows a dog very similar to today's Brittany Spaniel. The works of William Hogarth (1697–1794), Antoine Watteau (1684–1721), and Jean-Baptiste Greuze (1725–1805) among others, often included the dog. The painters A. F. Desportes (1661–1743) and Jean-Baptiste Oudry (1686–1755) specialized in painting the dog; Oudry produced a dog catalog of breed studies that has never been matched.

The next century gave rise to romantic paintings of dogs that sought to touch a sentimental chord. Subjects like the old dog pining at his master's grave, or a fat dog begging outside a bakery became the vogue. Alexandre Decamps (1803–1860) painted hounds, poachers' dogs, and the fat town dogs. Henri de Toulouse-Lautrec (1864–1901) painted the strays and street dogs of Paris. Impressionists Pierre Renoir (1841–1919) and Pierre Bonnard (1867–1947) enjoyed pet dogs, and painted them often. Pablo Picasso (1881–1973) had a Boxer named Jan.

It soon became fashionable for gentlemen to pose for portraits in sporting gear with their hunting dogs.

Fearsome creatures known as Cynocephali were monstermen with the heads of dogs who populated medieval legends; they were thought to worship Hecate, the goddess who could pacify the cruelest of dogs. St. Andrew had been instructed to preach the Gospel to these dog-men, and Cynocephali appear again and again in church manuscripts of the eleventh and twelfth centuries.

• Jean Baptiste Greuze (1725–1805), *A Girl Holding a Spaniel.*

THE REFINED DOG

Washington, D.C. gallery owner Kathleen Ewing is hard-pressed to name current artists that feature the dog. "There are so many!" she protests. Ewing is a dog lover who devotes a month every other summer to the "Biennial Dog Days Dog Show." The show features works by both well-known and amateur artists alike including Judy Sanchez, Robin Schwartz, Allan Janus, and Washington painter Frank Wright. William Wegman, Steve Szabo, and Constance Larabee have also contributed to the "Doggone" show. The entry fee is a minimum $5 donation to the Washington Animal Rescue League; a percentage of the price of any artwork sold is also contributed to this worthy cause.

SIGN OF THE DOG

Sir Edwin Landseer (1802–1873) was a favorite artist of Queen Victoria and Prince Albert, and he painted the royal family and their dogs. George Earl's early nineteenth-century painting of "Bob" can be found in the Dog Museum in St. Louis. Many of his paintings celebrated the sporting breeds. The English portrait painter Sir Joshua Reynolds (1723–1782) also included portraits of dogs in his work. More recently, painter Jon Van Zyle often features sled dogs in his Alaska scenes. World-renowned photographer William Wegman's (1942–) incredible portraits of his Weimaraner dogs "Man Ray" and "Fay Ray" are quite famous.

Today, dog lovers can choose from a wealth of doggy designs, canine cartoons, and pooch portraits. Prices vary from reasonable to outrageous. There are artists, some of whom advertise in the pages of *Dog Fancy* and *Dog World* magazines, who will make portraits of your special dog available in nearly every medium. But you don't have to commission an artist. You can use a camera to immortalize a favorite pooch in your own personal work of art.

• Above: Relief carving of a canine by Cellini Benvenuto (1500–1571). Above, right: The dog often appeared on family crests and coats of arms.

The dog represents fidelity, courage, affection, and generosity. The Dukes of Montmorency, Havray, and Crussol featured the head of a dog on the family crests, and military leaders of France had dogs on their Blazons to symbolize vigilance and courage. The Greyhound was found in the coats of arms of more than 400 noble families in nineteenth-century France, and has been the animal of honor for England's House of York since 1513.

"L'ordre du chien" (Order of the Dog) was a band of medieval knights who wore collars in the shape of a stag's head with a dog medallion that bore the motto *Vigiles* (vigilance). The order is thought to have been organized by Bouchard IV of Montmorency c. 1120.

Dog images were also found on seals and medals. Old European medallions and coins often showed hunters accompanied by dogs. Today in Spain, the two smallest bronze coins in circulation are called la perra chica or "little dog" and la perra gorda or "fat dog."

A DOG'S LIFE

Since the early 1900s, the Dachshund has been a symbol of that all-American passion, the hot dog. When Harry M. Stevens first put hot frankfurter sausages inside buns in 1906 at the Polo Grounds, home of the New York Giants, they became an immediate success. A sports cartoonist, T.A. "Tad" Dorgan, lampooned the popular food with a cartoon Dachshund inside the bun. It was Dorgan who coined the term "hot dog"; after all, both Dachshunds and frankfurters were red, long, and German. Stevens embraced "hot dog" as an advertising tool, but the term backfired when people got the idea that dog meat was in the food (it wasn't). Nevertheless, the term "hot dog" was banned from advertising by the local Chamber of Commerce. But nobody could bury such a good name forever and today the "wiener dog" and the "hot dog" are as popular as ever.

THE DOG IN MYTH AND SUPERSTITION

The night wind whips through the trees, bringing with it the eerie bell tones of a baying hound. Soon, the lonely serenade is answered by an echoing howl, and then another, and another still, until the macabre ensemble swells in awful, chilling harmony. Human hearts quicken and eyes cast about fearfully, until with chagrin they meet the curious, glistening gaze of the family dog stirring by the hearth. It has ever been so. Although a close friend to us, the dog nevertheless is not human and sometimes even acts as a reminder of all that we fear and cannot know.

Some early religions worshipped both the wolf and the dog, which have appeared in creation fables or as fantastic creatures with supernatural powers. In South America, some tribes believe that human life was first released from the underworld by a dog scratching up at the earth from below.

Vulcan, the Roman god of fire and metal, forged a bronze dog that slowly came to life under his divine breath. From this dog was born Cerberus, the watchdog of Hades. Cerberus lay chained to the gates of Hades, where he fawned on those who entered and devoured those who tried to escape. Cerberus had three heads: lion, wolf, and dog, with a mane of writhing snakes, a dragon's tail, and a Mastiff's body. The ancient Romans placed a cake in the hands of their dead to pacify Cerberus.

• Left: Dachshund. Above: A depiction of Cerberus, the most well-known mythological dog, on a Greek vase painting of the sixth century B.C.

THE REFINED DOG

The religions of a number of ancient cultures held that the passage between this world and the next was guarded by a huge dog. A Menominee Indian fable eared dog whose bark drives out the fiend from the souls of the good. lives won't be allowed to cross into the next world. The Icelandic goddess of the dead is Garm, the Dog of Hel; anyone who fed the needy while on earth will find bread in their hand with which to bribe Garm for safe passage. The sacred book of the Persians (the *Avesta*) tells of a rainbow bridge guarded by a yellow-eared dog whose bark drives out the fiend from the souls of the good.

The dog has also acted as a spiritual guide. At one time in Greenland, children who died were buried with the head of a dog—a trustworthy guide into the next world. To the early people of Mexico, the dog was the symbol of the "fire from heaven" (lightning) that upon striking the ground opens the way to hell; a pet dog was killed when its owner died, and its body was placed beside the body of its master so that the dead person could safely reach the other side.

Dogs have played a role in medicine as well. Early Spaniards believed a broth of dog kidney brought relief to one suffering a bloody flux, but eating the flesh of a bitch in heat could cause death. In Jamaica, hairless dogs called "fever dogs" were placed across the bodies of sick people to take away fever.

Shawnee Legend: Our Grandmother and her dog live close to the Land of the Dead, where she weaves a basket. When the basket is finished, the world will end; but each night while Our Grandmother sleeps, her little dog unravels the day's work and buys us a little more time.

Hindu folklore holds that a dog walking between pupil and teacher nullifies the day's lessons.

Dogs often suffered because of the superstitions associated with them. The ancient Chinese believed that demons feared black dogs; consequently, many black dogs were sacrificed so that their blood could be sprinkled to exorcise demons. During the Middle Ages in Europe, a similar belief fostered the practice of smearing the blood of black dogs on the walls of the home to protect the householder from demonic possession. In Brittany, elaborate rites supposedly forced wicked souls into black dogs, which were then ceremoniously destroyed.

But the dog has also been considered a lucky mascot. One superstition holds that if a black dog follows you home, good luck is sure to come after. Another says that to dream of a black dog or to see the likeness of a dog in the fire are both signs that a friend is near.

It is said that dreaming of dogs may indicate any number of things. Dreaming of traveling alone with a dog following you signifies steadfast friends and successful undertakings; dreaming of a friendly white dog is an omen of early marriage for a woman; and a dream of swimming dogs predicts happiness and fortune. To dream that a dog snuggles up to you indicates great gain and constant friendships, and a dream of owning a fine dog indicates future wealth.

But to dream that a Bloodhound is tracking you portends a future temptation that may mean your

A DOG'S LIFE

downfall. A dream of vicious dogs denotes enemies and perpetual bad luck, and a dog biting you in your dreams prophesizes a disagreeable companion, either in business or marriage.

South American lore tells of dog-demons that sit in judgment of human souls. Tezcatlipoca is the Aztec Prince of the underworld in the Mexican *Book of the Dead*. He has powers over both life and death, is a bringer of disease and pestilence, and often appears as a dog or Coyote. Zotz is a huge winged creature with the head of a dog that lives in the darkest regions of caves, according to ancient Mayan scriptures. Condemned souls must travel through the House of Bats, so that Zotz may receive his daily allotment of blood.

Kludde is an evil, Belgian goblin, well known in Brabant and Flanders. By some he is known as Waternix, while in the countryside he is feared as a werewolf. Kludde has the power to take the form of any animal he chooses, but most often appears as a large winged black dog that walks on its hind legs. He plays brutal tricks on people, usually around twilight, knocking them down and then disappearing. One can hear the chain about his neck clanking and can recognize him by the two small blue flames that hover about his head.

To hear barking dogs predicts depressing news. Dogs growling and fighting portends one will be overcome by enemies. The baying of a dog foretells a death.

During the Salem witch trials in Massachusetts (1692–1693), one of the self-confessed witches claimed the Devil appeared to her in the shape of a brown dog and a spotted female dog. Scottish folk tales mention witches worshipping a small black dog sitting on a rock. Freemasons were believed to have sold their souls to the Devil, who appeared to them in the form of a black Poodle.

unaware of such curses have experienced them. The fierce "Black Dog of Leeds" dates from the fifteenth century and is considered a portent of doom. This dog is thought to be the ghost of Henry VI's aunt, who was imprisoned in the castle for practicing witchcraft. The infamous Newgate Prison was said to have its own ghostly white dog that appeared at the gates before every execution.

Ghost Dogs

Not all visitations of ghostly dogs are of a sinister nature. Whenever a beloved pet dies, it's natural to mourn. Some dogs are said to be reluctant to be separated from their masters, even by death. Stories abound of ghostly barking and whining, spectral paws treading old, familiar paths, and phantom images lingering near loved ones.

Albert Payson Terhune, renowned writer of dog stories, had a favorite mixed-breed dog named Rex. Rex was a big, tan, short-haired dog with a distinctive scar on his face. Rex was in the habit of staring in through the window when the Terhune family sat down

Even the fictional Sherlock Holmes had a run-in with a spectral canine, in the famous tale *The Hound of the Baskervilles*; the story hinged upon the legend of the giant hound that always appeared before the death of a member of the Baskerville family.

Fiction may have its basis in fact. Even those

- Above: In this illustration of Arthur Conan Doyle's famous ghostly canine, Sherlock Holmes and the ever faithful Watson observe the Hound of the Baskervilles from a safe vantage point.

In Irish folklore, the Devil's dog waits for sinners to die so he can chase and torment the wicked souls.

THE REFINED DOG

to dinner. A short time after Rex died in 1916, the Reverend Appleton Grannis, an old friend of the family, came to visit. The Reverend hadn't seen the Terhunes in years and had never met Rex. Nevertheless, while in the dining room, Grannis suddenly exclaimed to Terhune that a strange dog was staring in the window at them. The dog disappeared before Terhune could turn around and see it, but Grannis described Rex perfectly, right down to the distinguishing scar on the dog's face. Two years later, another Terhune family friend swore he saw Rex lying at his feet when he visited the farm.

Are the ghosts of departed canines merely figments of human imagination? Other dogs apparently don't think so. Terhune noted that for years one of his other dogs refused to walk over ground that had been one of Rex's favorite spots.

Pierre van Paasen, a Dutch writer, tells of a black ghost dog that lived in his house and often appeared to walk past him on the stairs. One day Paasen brought two live dogs into the house. On this occasion, he did not see the ghost dog himself, but heard and watched a horrendous fight between the two live dogs and the specter. The ghost dog won.

Such ghost dogs occasionally intervene in the life of the living to good effect. Leeds Castle, a medieval fortress in the Kentish countryside near Maidstone, England, has at least three ghost dogs, and one actually saved a life. A visitor perched in a bay-window seat in a room located high over the moat saw a black dog walking across the room. She thought it was a real dog until it disappeared into the wall. Surprised, the woman rose from her seat to investigate; abruptly, the bay window cracked and fell apart, dropping into the water below with a crash. Had she not risen to follow the mysterious ghost dog, the woman would have plunged to her death.

Psychic Dogs

Is your dog psychic? Does he or she read your mind? When you decide to go for a walk, does Princess race excitedly to your side even before you've left your chair? Does Pepper send messages to you when he stares deeply, expectantly, into your eyes, until you somehow *know* his ball has fallen behind furniture beyond doggy reach?

Dr. Aristide Esser, psychiatrist and neurologist, says, "There is no doubt in my mind that some dogs, particularly those with a close relationship with their owners, have highly developed ESP." Esser conducted experiments in 1975 at Rockland State Hospital in New York, using copper-lined chambers that were sound- and vibration-proof located in different areas of the hospital. The human was placed in one chamber, his or her canine in the other. When one man acted out shooting game, his Beagles in the distant chamber went crazy, barking and whining with excitement as if they were

- Above: Black dogs like the Chow were often persecuted by the superstitious.

A DOG'S LIFE
50

experiencing a real hunting trip. In another experiment, a woman was unexpectedly confronted with an angry, threatening man; her Boxer in the other box registered a sharp increase in heart rate at the same time.

Psychic dogs seem to "know" things in advance, or receive "messages" over long distances. Hunters' dogs even seem able to predict whether a shot will be successful or not. Everyone who has lived with a dog has experienced this unsettling phenomenon. With a few dogs, the talent is extraordinary.

Dogs often use their abilities to save their owners' lives. In his book, *The Secret Life of Animals*, Joseph Wilder cites extraordinary examples of psychic activities in pets. A setter named Redsy one day refused to get in the boat to accompany her master on a fishing trip. The weather looked perfect, but the dog steadfastly refused to obey her master. Finally, the man yielded to Redsy's barked protest and canceled the day's fishing. An hour later, the great hurricane of 1938 blew in, and more than 600 human lives were lost.

Here's another example. On a camping trip, Mrs. Kearns' dog Buffy, a Keeshund, became nearly crazed when they set up camp in a small valley. Finally, Mrs. Kearns gave in to Buffy's wild insistence, and they moved the camp to a hillside. Three campers drowned that night in a flash flood after camping in the valley where Buffy had sounded her warning.

Some dogs have been able to locate people even when separated by long distances. This inexplicable talent, called "psi-trailing," has been noted for centuries, even immortalized in such classic stories as *The Incredible Journey* by Sheila Burnford and *Lassie Come-Home* by Eric Knight.

One of the best authenticated examples of canine psi-trailing is the true story of Bobbie. Bobbie accompanied his family on vacation. They were driving east from their home in Oregon. When they reached Wolcott, Indiana, Bobbie spied a dog fight and leaped through the car window to join the fray. By the time the car stopped, the local dogs had suspended their fight long enough to chase the intruder out of sight. A search was mounted, but Bobbie could not be found. His family finally gave up, and reluctantly returned to Oregon, using a totally different route that passed through Mexico.

Six months later, an exhausted, bony, and half-starved Bobbie arrived at his home in Oregon. Affidavits by the Humane Society and others along the way proved that Bobbie didn't retrace the route through Indiana, nor did he follow the path through Mexico; Bobbie struck out straight for Oregon, traveling through the Rocky Mountains to be reunited with the family he loved.

● Below: Beaumaris, a Golden Retriever puppy.

THE REFINED DOG

DOG STARS

Dogs have been associated with performing probably as long as humans have sought to entertain themselves. Acrobatic dogs, juggling dogs, tightrope-walking dogs, clown dogs, football- and frisbee-playing dogs have all amused and amazed circus-goers for centuries. With the advent of films and television, the dog got its chance to really shine.

One of the earliest canine stars was Rin Tin Tin (Rinty), a German Shepherd. As a puppy, Rinty was found by Lee Duncan in a trench in France during World War I. Rinty became a Warner Brothers film star in the 1920s (his first film was *The Night Cry*). This exceptional dog was voted the most popular film performer in 1926. When he died in 1932, his four sons carried on the tradition. Rinty number four was the star of the television series *Rin Tin Tin*, for which in 1958 and 1959 he won the Patsy, an award given to animal actors by the American Humane Association.

German Shepherds have appeared in not only the *Rin Tin Tin* series, but also starred in *The Littlest Hobo* and *The Adventures of Champion*. The television roles of "Bullet," the Wonder Dog on *The Roy Rogers Show,* and the bionic dog Max in *The Bionic Woman* were also played by German Shepherds.

Collie popularity surged with the debut of another great canine star. Pal belonged to trainer Rudd Weatherwax; Pal was the first dog to play the role of "Lassie" and starred in the movie *Lassie Come-Home* in 1943. Pal lived to be nineteen years old, and Pal Jr.

- Right: Skippy, shown here with William Powell and Myrna Loy, starred in *The Thin Man* films.

played Lassie on the television show. All "Lassies" have been male Collies. Lassie won so many Patsy awards that the dog was finally barred from competing.

In 1958, a dog named Spike won the Patsy for his title role in *Old Yeller*. Spike also played the dog that accompanied *The Westerner*. When the Dashiell Hammett novel *The Thin Man* was turned into a movie series, a Wire-Haired Terrier named Skippy played the part of "Asta." In 1961, Tramp, the Old English Sheepdog on the television show *My Three Sons* won the Patsy. A Great Dane named Duke brought his breed recognition when he played the title role in *The Ugly Dachshund*.

Tundra the Samoyed is a modern dog star. She lives with her trainer/agent Ted Baer, and has had more than sixty television and film appearances, including commercials, an appearance on *The Love Boat,* and a role in the film *Against All Odds*. Tundra knows 200 commands and seventy hand signals. In one commercial, Tundra actually drops in the coffee filter followed by the coffee, then watches it drip, and finally pours a cup. Tundra has won the Patsy Award, and is also honored in the Dog Museum in St. Louis, Missouri.

Dogs don't need a pedigree to make it in the movies. Regular mutts have often stolen the show. It matters little if your dog has a pedigree or incorporates numerous breeds in its ancestry. Whether Fluffy has mastered 100 tricks or none at all, we each know our dog is as gifted and handsome as any of the celebrated canines before the camera.

BEST FRIENDS

Historically, the dog's most important role was as worker—hunter, shepherd, protector, and draft animal. Today, most dogs no longer perform the tasks for which they were originally bred; the dog is usually a companion. But this is not necessarily canine choice; many dogs still yearn for the rewards of challenging work, and some are much more than "just a pretty face."

A-Hunting We Will Go

Spaniels, hounds, terriers, pointers, and retrievers were all bred with a yen for the smells, the thrill, and the joy of pursuit, and the pride of retrieval. Hunting dogs have been loved and celebrated in story and fable.

One of the oldest hunting breeds, the Greyhound, has found a new sport at which to excel. At the beginning of the twentieth century, an engineer named Owen Smith came up with the idea of Greyhound stadium racing, and today the Greyhound is almost exclusively a race dog, running an incredible 40 to 45 miles (64-72km) per hour.

Lure coursing is a sport that simulates hunting for live game. Sight-hound breeds such as the Afghan Hound, Whippet, Borzoi, Saluki, and others are run in open fields in trios or pairs. The dogs' goal is to work as a team to catch the plastic lure. Speed, follow, enthusiasm, agility, and endurance are tested in these exciting contests.

In 1878, Charles Burden's Foxhound, Old Drum, was thought by many to be the best hunting dog in America. When Burden's neighbor lost several sheep to pillaging animals, he swore to kill the next dog seen on his land. Burden was devastated when he found Old Drum shot dead. Although he couldn't prove it, he was certain the neighbor had shot his dog, and filed suit for the maximum damages allowed—$50. Burden lost and appealed the case again and again until it finally reached the Missouri Supreme Court. There, he managed to obtain the services of attorney George Graham Vest, whose spontaneous oration "Tribute to a Dog" shamed the court and jury into awarding Burden compensation. From this famous speech came the saying, "The dog is man's best friend." Eighty years later, a statue in memory of Old Drum was placed on the Johnson County Courthouse lawn.

- Above: This antique print portrays pointers doing what they do best—sniffing out prey.

THE REFINED DOG

• Below: A Border Collie named Tweed resting comfortably on a pile of freshly sheared sheep wool.

Terriers are another old hunting breed rarely used for that purpose today. The American Working Terrier Association has developed a safe field trial program to test the terriers' working instincts. Trials known as "digs" or "go-to-grounds" utilize buried wood-lined boxes to form tunnels. Live rats in protective cages at the end of the boxes supply the scent and bait to induce the dogs to "hunt." The experienced tame rats are totally unconcerned; they know there's no danger. The dogs work against the clock, and must run into the tunnel and show interest in obtaining the "prey."

The "Spit Dog" was used in England in the 1400s to help cook meat. A rope-and-pulley mechanism leading from the roasting spit to a drum-shaped wooden cage mounted on the wall was the world for many small dogs. These dogs, usually hyperactive terriers, were locked in the cage and made to run. As the cage revolved, the spit was cranked, and the meat was roasted evenly.

Shepherds and Sheepdogs

From the hardy, diminutive Shetland Sheepdog to the massive Newfoundland, shepherd dogs share an inbred need to herd and protect. Their talent for moving seas of animals by cajoling and intimidation is impressive. Shepherds also must be fierce enough to face down foxes, wolves, and other predators to protect their charges. The instinct is so ingrained that even dogs that have never seen a sheep, cow, or reindeer will nonetheless "ride herd" on the children or other pets in their home. Traditionally, the shepherd dog protects and the sheepdog herds. However, there are a wide range of dogs that to a large extent fit both bills.

Draft Dogs

In the past, many large dogs were used to pull loads; both the Rottweiler and the St. Bernard were bred as draft animals. Today, Belgium, Switzerland, Holland, and some German provinces still use dogs for this purpose, but the practice is carefully regulated. The sight of "Man's Best Friend" straining and grunting with its tongue hanging out is too pathetic a sight for many countries to sanction such labor.

In the United States, carting has become more an amusing pastime than actual labor for the dog. Dogs carry backpacks for hikers, pull baby carriages, and are often seen with dogcarts in local parades. The Newfoundland Club of America offers a Draft Dog title, and dogs of any size may compete in weight-pull contests. Dogs are judged on the percentage of body weight they can pull, and compete in separate weight classes.

Sled dogs like the Malamute and Husky usually work in packs or teams; the pack instinct rates more highly in them than in perhaps any other breeds. These dogs must be able to travel long distances in temperatures as low as 40 degrees below zero and in gale-force winds.

A DOG'S LIFE

Rowdy of Nome was a Malamute that helped open the public's eyes to the wonders of his breed. He participated in the first Byrd Antarctic expedition, a 1600-mile (2560km) trek by dogsled across unknown Antarctic territory. Rowdy became famous as the "Mayor of Dogtown," and for years his portrait headed the Alaskan Malamute column in the American Kennel Club Gazette. *Rowdy had the honor of unveiling the Admiral Byrd Memorial to sled dogs and lived to a venerable age of twenty.*

Sled dogs are still important in the Far North, but are also trained by enthusiasts fot the pure recreation of the sport. The magazine *Mushing,* available from Stellar Communications, Inc., P.O. Box 149, Ester, AK 99725, covers all aspects of dogsledding, and *Dog Fancy* and *Dog World* magazines occasionally offer articles on the subject.

Skijoring is a major competitive sport in northern Europe, where dogs pull a small light sled with a skier behind. In America, skijoring is a modified sport in which harnessed sled dogs pull a cross-country skier.

Law-Enforcement Dogs

The use of police dogs in London began informally in the nineteenth century when pets accompanied officer/owners on patrol. In 1938, a training school opened in England and in 1953, the training school for the Metropolitan Police Dog Section was moved to the Dog Training Establishment in Keston, Kent County. German Shepherds are used most often for law enforcement, but Labradors, Springer Spaniels, Weimaraners, Bouvier des Flandres, Airedales, Rottweilers, and Dobermans are used as well.

The number of law-enforcement dogs is increasing. Keen senses of smell and hearing make dogs priceless time-savers—and increase the safety of police officers. The dog also provides a deterrent to crime. Jim Barnes, a K-9 dog trainer and sheriff's deputy, notes, "You can call back a dog if the person gives up, but you can't call back a bullet."

Ollie was a throwaway pet abandoned at the pound. When Ollie had trouble breathing and was x-rayed, a puppy-size flea collar was discovered embedded in his neck. United States Customs officers that had rescued the German Shepherd–Husky mix had the collar surgically removed. Today Ollie is an enthusiastic and valued member of the United States Customs' drug-sniffing canine team.

• Below: German Shepherds form strong bonds with human partners.

THE REFINED DOG

55

Edinburgh's "Bob" was an army mascot from 1853 to 1860, and won a medal in the Crimean War. Former Scottish United Services Museum curator Major H.P.E. Pereira wrote, "He is said to have shown a complete disregard for cannonballs and even chased them. More than once he was reported to have burned his nose on a hot one he did not treat with respect!"

- Right: Coast Guard war dogs and their trainers on guard and scout detail. These "off-leash" dogs have been trained to bring in prisoners, make rounds unescorted, and alert their masters when they detect anything suspicious.

Military Dogs

The military "devouring dogs" of the ancients have evolved into dogs with specialized skills similar to those of police dogs. These dogs are trained to work in the worst conditions: they run under bullet fire, and even have been parachuted into inaccessible areas. Between 1940 and 1945, eighteen dogs were decorated by the British military. Scout dogs were used in the Vietnam War; they no longer exist in the military, but will forever live on in the memory of the men whose lives they saved.

Edinburgh Castle's Cemetery for Soldiers' Dogs is a fitting memorial to the countless canines that have followed their masters into war. Tombstones commemorate Gyp, Yum Yum, Scamp, Major, and others. Dogs were laid to rest there from 1742 to 1982, and no one knows for certain just how many dogs are buried in the cemetery.

Often, lonely soldiers far from home adopt stray dogs. Sadly, many of these dogs are abandoned to suffer, and slowly die when their masters return home. When Staff Sergeant Ed Lynde rescued a skin-and-bones puppy from an enemy bunker in Iraq during the Gulf War, everyone kept telling him there was no way for him to bring "Sergeant Sandy" back home. Lynde happily proved them wrong; he raised the necessary funds, tracked down a veterinarian 300 miles (480km) away to complete the forms, and in mid-May 1991, the five-month-old puppy arrived in Oklahoma. Sergeant Sandy stood on the front lawn of Lynde's house and barked loudly at the first tree she'd ever seen in her short, hectic life.

Military dogs have acted as watch dogs, guard dogs, patrol dogs, message dogs, mine-detecting dogs, and ambulance dogs. Corky the Beagle works for the United States Navy uncovering illegal drugs and is known as the best drug-detector dog in the military.

A DOG'S LIFE

[The pig] had an appetite at the end of a rope, [while the truffle dog] is an artiste to all appearances which is studious in dedicating itself to its art.

—Rudyard Kipling

Sniffers

The dog possesses an incredible sense of smell. Pigs were originally used to sniff out truffles, but dogs were considered superior because they weren't tempted to eat the delicacy once it was found. Even Louis XV of France enjoyed hunting truffles with his favorite dog. Dogs were also used to sniff out and retrieve wild birds' eggs.

Today dogs are trained to sniff out and detect an astounding variety of items, from termites and other pests to the hydrocarbons often used by arsonists to set fires.

Search and Rescue Dogs

The search-and-rescue (SAR) dog has been around for centuries. In 1750, St. Bernard dogs were used by monks as guides through the soft, treacherous snow of the Alps. Often, these noble dogs saved human lives. Both St. Bernards and Pyrenean Mountain Dogs have historically been used to find and rescue wayward travelers caught in snowstorms or avalanches.

Today, The Swiss Société Cynologique has worked to develop dogs able to find missing or even hidden people, dead or alive. These dogs are used not only for avalanche work, but also in the aftermath of earthquakes, floods, and other natural disasters.

Most SAR teams are not paid for their important work; dogs and human partners are volunteers dedicated to service. The individual dog is more important than the specific breed, but the most common dogs used for SAR are German Shepherds, Golden Retrievers, Labradors, Dobermans, and mixed breeds that have inherited sporting and herding traits.

• Above: St. Bernard.

THE REFINED DOG

57

- Below: Lee Crane depends on his guide dog "Hooter."

Assistance Dogs

Dogs have been of extraordinary help to people in the past, and never more so as when partnered with physically challenged individuals. Dogs joyfully become our eyes, our ears, even our legs and hands, and guide us through the perils of emotional and mental anguish; they ask of us only love in return.

After World War I, the German government began training dogs as guides for soldiers blinded during the war. When American Dorothy Eustis traveled to Switzerland to breed and train German Shepherd dogs, she saw such a dog and sent a letter describing what she had seen to *The Saturday Evening Post*. A young blind American man named Morris Frank was greatly interested in the concept and convinced Mrs. Eustis to train such a dog for him. Frank traveled to Switzerland in April 1928, and was presented with a female German

Guide Dogs for the Blind of Great Britain was founded in 1931 by Muriel Cooke and Lady Kitty Ritson, breeders and trainers of Alsatians (German Shepherds), and Mr. Musgrave Frankland of the National Institute for the Blind. Captain Liakhoff was selected to be a trainer by Dorothy Eustis, who consulted the budding organization. Liakhoff was later awarded the Order of the British Empire for this important work.

Guide dogs are known by their special harness and handle; signal dogs wear a blaze orange collar; service and therapy dogs wear identification as well. Most laws allow assistance dogs open access to wherever their partners must go, including planes, restaurants, stores, and theaters.

Shepherd, which he promptly named Buddy. Frank and Buddy were instrumental in getting the word out about the wonderful possibilities of guide dogs. The Seeing Eye organization opened in Nashville, Tennessee, in 1928, and a year later moved to New Jersey.

Guide dogs virtually become the eyes of their human companions, in a partnership that must be witnessed to be believed. The first guide dog in Australia was named Beau. Beau learned the meaning and locations of many kinds of shops, so that his mistress had only to say "cake-shop," "butcher," or "post office" to be guided to the appropriate place. Guide dogs not only guide, but also protect their companions. Dixie, a Labrador Retriever, has twice shielded her owner Doreen Cox from pickpockets, and once stopped her from falling down an open elevator shaft. To the dog, it's all in a day's work.

In 1974, a hearing-impaired woman lost a dog that had learned to be her "ears" over the years. She asked the Minnesota Humane Society to train another dog, and the society contacted Agnes McGrath, who selected and trained the first dog to aid the hearing-impaired.

A DOG'S LIFE
58

Signal dogs are trained to hear and alert owners to important sounds, such as the doorbell, alarm clock, crying baby, fire alarm, siren, and the like. Each dog's training is matched to the future owner's individual needs. All dogs are trained to be persistent; a signal dog must not give up until its human partner investigates the source of the sound.

The smaller breeds are typically used as signal dogs because they alert by touch, usually jumping against or on their owner. Large dogs are certainly capable of the job, but having a Newfoundland jumping into your lap is quite a different experience than having a Chihuahua do so. Mixed breeds are often used as signal dogs, as are "throwaway" animals that are rescued from pounds.

Sadie the Collie was a stray rescued by the Hearing Ear Dog Program of West Boylston, Massachusetts. She proved her worth many times over when she saved her owner Mary Lou Steger and her children from a fire in their home. A Chihuahua-mix signal dog named Chico insisted that his hearing-impaired owner, Elizabeth Smith of Watertown, Massachusetts, leave a city bus; the roof of the bus was on fire. These dogs are carefully trained, but also must know when to break the rules. Dude, a signal dog trained by International Hearing Dog of Colorado, was taught not to bark—but barked until help arrived when his owner suffered a severe heart attack. Every signal dog is a hero twenty-four hours a day, 365 days a year, just by giving the precious gifts of independence and peace of mind to their owners.

Bonnie Bergin, founder of Canine Companions for Independence (CCI), noticed while teaching in Asia that burros were being used by some people to stay independent who otherwise might have been institutionalized due to physical problems. In 1976, she placed the first CCI-trained dog: a black Labrador named Abdul transformed Kerrie Knause's life from around-the-clock care to one of freedom.

• Above: German Shepherd.

THE REFINED DOG

Support Dogs for the Handicapped of St. Louis, Missouri, found Jocko, a Great Dane/Retriever cross, at a local pound; he had been dumped on Interstate 44. Jocko is now the organization's ambassador and demo-dog.

Organizations like CCI train extraordinary dogs for service with physically challenged individuals. These dogs learn to pull wheelchairs, push elevator buttons, give checks to bank tellers, operate wheelchair lifts in vehicles, retrieve dropped items, answer the phone, and generally give support to disabled individuals wherever needed.

Nancy Vida trained a service dog for her sister, who was afflicted with multiple sclerosis. When enormous interest was generated by her sister's dog, Nancy founded D.O.G.S. for the Handicapped with several other dog trainers in 1989. D.O.G.S. (Devoted, Obedient, Giving, Serving) does not charge clients and operates solely on donations. Larger, older organizations often have waiting lists of two years or more. But smaller groups like D.O.G.S. may be able to provide dogs within six months to qualified individuals.

One of the first dogs trained and placed by D.O.G.S. was Mac. Today, Anne Mareno and Mac are inseparable. When Anne recently underwent electronic therapy at Allied Services in Scranton, Pennsylvania, in the hopes of walking again, Mac was the first service dog allowed into the program. Today, Mac remains faithfully at Anne's side, supporting her as she successfully regains her ability to walk.

CCI also trains social or therapy dogs for work known as Pet-Facilitated Therapy. Therapy dogs became popular in the 1980s, when it was discovered that people who keep dogs live longer than those who don't; the calming influence of a pet reduces blood pressure and may help may health problems. Furthermore, dogs seem able to touch emotionally disturbed individuals on a level not otherwise possible.

Therapy dogs are chosen for their even temperament and affectionate nature, and bring joy, comfort, and therapeutic rehabilitation to many people who suffer from mental or emotional difficulties. Therapy dogs perform such valuable services as assisting in preschools for children with development disorders and working in nursing-home programs to brighten the lives of elderly residents.

There is no psychiatrist in the world like a puppy licking your face.

—Bern Williams

Jack Butrick and his red Doberman, Stormy, became involved with Therapy Dogs International, located in Hillside, New Jersey. Stormy was happy to perform his obedience work and clown tricks for everyone. During one nursing-home visit, an elderly man petted and talked enthusiastically to Stormy and human companions; it was the first time he had spoken in months. Although Stormy later lost his right front leg to cancer, the dog refused to cut back his work on the oncology floor at Children's Hospital in Denver. "Those little guys just loved that big brave dog," said Butrick. Stormy died nine months after his leg was amputated, but in his short six-and-a-half-year life he brought joy and laughter to ease the suffering and pain of more human friends than can be counted.

Assistance dogs that perform duties with a wag of the tail on a daily basis are miracles to their handlers. These dogs are more than pets; they make independence and a normal life possible. Assistance dogs combine the dogs' willing devotion with the determination of the human spirit, and together they create magic.

Assistance Dogs are not for everyone; applicants for the dogs are rigorously screened. Not every dog chosen for training works out, either; however, such dogs are usually easily placed in homes because their training makes them ideal pets. Dogs that reach retirement age (which varies according to program and individual dog) are either allowed to continue to live with their partners, or are found retirement homes.

A large number of training centers for assistance dogs are located throughout the world. The following represents only a small sampling; contact health-services organizations or humane associations for information on training centers in your area.

CCI
4350 Occidental Road
P.O. Box 446
Santa Rosa, CA 95402-0446

Dogs for the Handicapped, Inc.
Nancy Vida
P.O. Box 215
Elkhart, IN 46515-0215
(219) 293-5649

Guide Dog Association of New South Wales
77 Deepfield Road
Catherine Field, NSW 2171
Sydney, Australia
02-606-6616

Guide Dogs for the Blind
9 Park Street
Windsor, Berkshire
England SL4 1LU
753-855-711

Hearing Ear Dogs of Canada
P.O. Box 907
Oakville, Ontario
Canada, L6J 5E8
(416) 842-7344

International Hearing Dog, Inc.
5901 East 89th Avenue
Henderson, Colorado 80640
(303) 287-3277

Support Dogs for the Handicapped, Inc.
301 Sovereign Court Street
St. Louis, Missouri 63011
(314) 394-6163

• Above: Labrador Retrievers make excellent guide dogs.

THE REFINED DOG

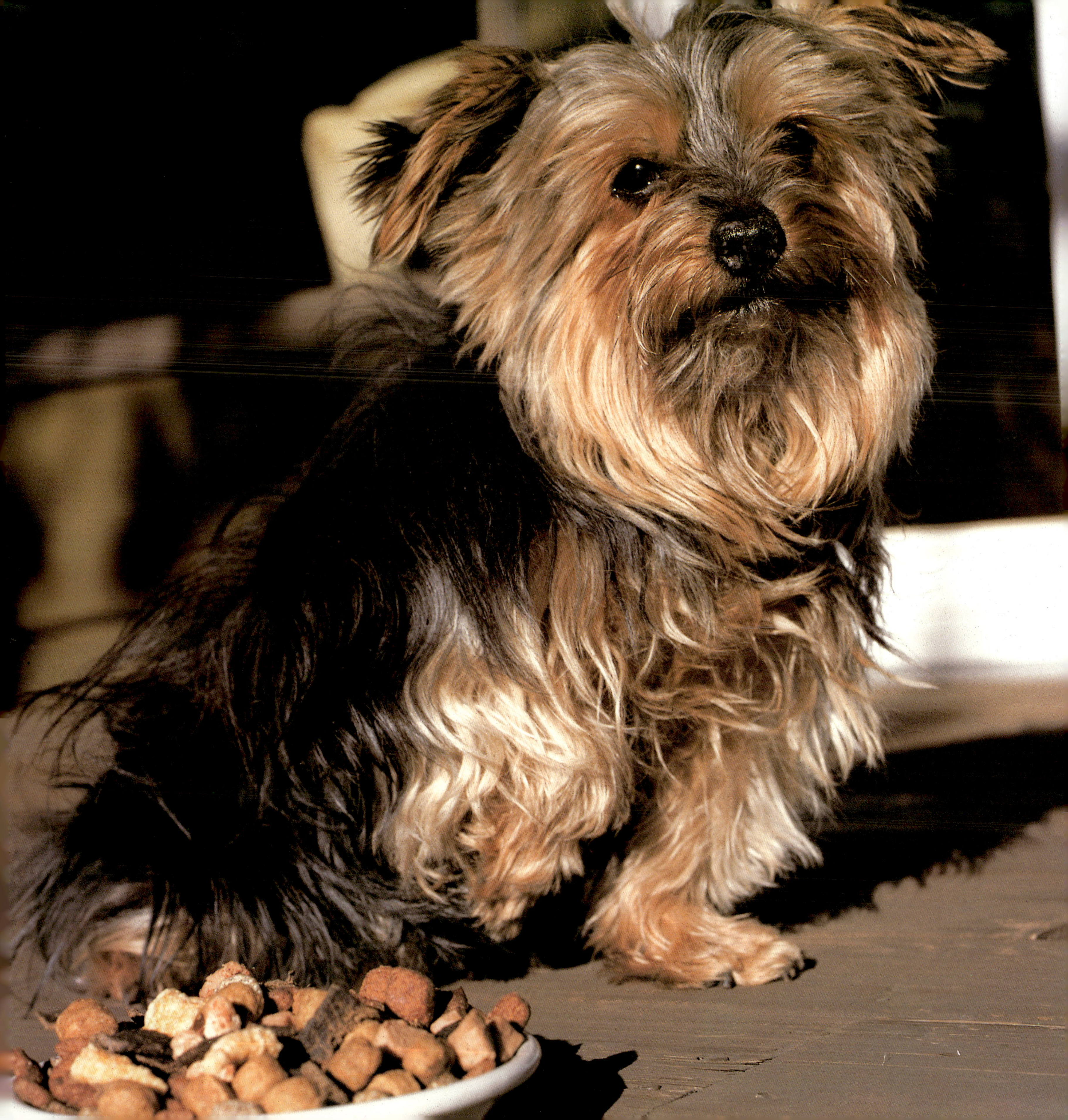

Shave one cat, ten cats, a hundred cats...and you will always be left with a cat, morphologically identical with all the others. With dogs, it is quite a different matter.

—*Fernand Mery,*
The Dog, 1968

CHAPTER THREE

IT'S A DOG'S LIFE

THE PHYSICAL DOG

The dog is built for endurance and strength. Unlike any other animal (except humans and monkeys), dogs are blessed with generous facial muscles that offer an incredible mobility of expression. Indeed, its whimsical face has long endeared the dog to man. Dogs grin at us when pleased, and their furrowed brows display a distinctly perplexed expression.

Although the structure of all canine skeletons is identical, size and shape of individual bones varies from breed to breed. For instance, the German Shepherd's jaws are long and wolfy, but those of the Pekingese are short and wide. All dog skeletons contain about 319 individual bones.

How can a dog fold itself double to scratch that itch at the base of its tail, or sleep pretzeled into an area

• Opposite: Yorkshire Terrier.

THE SKELETON

Illustration labels: PELVIC GIRDLE, SACRUM, LUMBAR VERTEBRAE, THORACIC VERTEBRAE, ALTAS, SKULL, SCAPULA, CERVICAL VERTEBRAE, ACETALULUM (HIP JOINT), FEMUR, HUMERUS, TAIL (CAUDAL VERTEVRAE), STERNUM, PATELLA, RIB, TIBIA, RADIUS, FIBULA, ULNA, CARPALS, TARSALS, METACARPALS, METATARSALS, PHALANGES, PHALANGES

Illustration by Linda Krause

Toes and Claws

Theoretically, all dogs have five toes on each of their front feet (counting the dew-claw), and four on the hind. Each toe has a claw made of keratin that grows constantly. Claws protect the toes and are used to scratch and dig; although they may be worn down through work or play, many must be trimmed for comfort and should clear the floor when the dog is standing. Long, untrimmed nails catch in carpeting and become tangled in bedding. Often toenails curl as they grow, making it difficult for the dog to walk, and may even grow into the flesh of the toe itself.

Puppies' and tiny dogs' nails may be trimmed with human nail clippers or very sharp scissors; larger dogs need heavy trimmers designed for dog nails (such as guillotine-type). Don't forget dew claws, and never cut into the pink "quick;" this contains nerves and blood vessels. Cut only white or clear tips of the nails, which can be trimmed without pain, and trim no closer than $1/10$ inch (25mm) to the pink portion. Some pigmented nails hide the quick. In this case, hold trimmers so the nail is cut parallel to and only slightly shorter than the level of the toe pad; generally, the quick doesn't grow that far. If you accidentally "quick" the nail, a styptic pencil will stop the bleeding. Remember, the more comfortable you make the procedure, the less trouble it will be for all concerned.

Polydactylism is the presence of extra toes, usually of the "dew" claw (thumb toe) located well up the sides of the leg. Double dew claws are required in the Briard and Great Pyrenees, but in other breeds are often surgically removed.

barely big enough to breathe? Dogs have five more vertebrae than we do; the extras are located behind the shoulder blades, and add flexibility and mobility. A dog's neck contains seven cervical vertebrae, enabling them to turn nearly 180 degrees to look behind themselves. Dogs have thirteen thoracic, seven lumbar, and three sacral vertebrae, with up to twenty-two additional vertebrae making up the tail.

Instead of a rigid collar bone, dogs have only a remnant of cartilage, and the shoulder blades are on their sides, which gives them a longer stride in running. All dogs are "digitigrade"; that is, they walk on their toes, which also lengthens their stride.

A DOG'S LIFE

The Council of the Royal College of Veterinary Surgeons, the Council of Europe, and the British government all oppose tail docking, and it's against the law in Sweden to trim a dog's tail for cosmetic reasons. Ear cropping is illegal in England, West Germany, and several Canadian provinces.

Cropping and Docking

In America, several breed specifications call for a docked tail and/or cropped ears. In the eighteenth century, docking a dog's tail was thought to prevent rabies, and more recently, bob-tailed dogs were considered working dogs and weren't taxed. Ears were cut close to the head to keep them from being torn during work or by adversaries.

Cropping is an expensive, painful procedure performed on nine to twelve-week-old puppies. While under anesthesia, the dog's ear leather is surgically cut and shaped so the ears stand erect. Ears are bandaged and stretched with "splints" that mold the ear to the cosmetically approved shape. Even when the wounds are healed, the process of rebandaging and splinting may take up to six months, and is not always successful. Tail docking is typically performed without anesthesia when puppies are three to five days old; depending on the breed, some or most of the tail is chopped off with scissors, thereby "cutting off" much of the canine "tail semaphore" communication.

Fur and Shedding

Growth of a dog's fur is cyclical; it grows for short periods, rests, then dries and is shed. Length of the cycle varies with the breed, but on average it takes about 130 days to grow a coat. Changes in surrounding light trigger the shedding cycle; the more exposure to light, the more your dog will shed. House dogs exposed to long hours of artificial light seem to shed nearly year-round.

Most dogs shed at least yearly, and some twice a year. Shed dog hair is magnetically attracted to our best clothes; consequently, we carry a little bit of our dogs with us wherever we go.

• Above: Samoyed puppy. Breeds with heavy "double coats" (Chow, Samoyed, and others) shed cottony undercoats in clumpy patches, and may look a bit "moth-eaten" unless regularly groomed.

IT'S A DOG'S LIFE

Today, controversy rages over whether such cosmetic surgery is valid. Erect ears are prone to fewer infections, and docked tails may prevent potential damage to working and hunting canines; however, in most cases, conformity to tradition is the true motivation for the alterations. Show dogs have little chance of success unless they have been trimmed and docked according to accepted standards. Until breed clubs alter their standards and forbid the practice of cropping and docking, this outmoded and cruel custom will continue.

Eating and Drinking

All adult dogs have twelve incisors, four carnassials, twelve premolars, ten molars, and four canine teeth. Dogs don't chew; food is only roughly chopped, and the wide, extensible esophagus allows large portions to be swallowed. Food stays in the stomach a relatively long time. Perhaps that's why dogs like to find a good spot to sleep following every meal. To drink, a dog curls its tongue into a spoon shape to scoop liquid, and laps water into the back of the mouth. They swallow after every two to three laps.

The dog's sense of taste is probably as discriminating as a human's. Dogs can discern salty, bitter, acidic, and sweet tastes, and may get in trouble by overindulging a sweet tooth. In tests, smaller breed dogs show stronger and more taste preferences than larger breeds. Perhaps the stereotypical finicky toy dog isn't farfetched at all.

The saliva of dogs is alkaline and contains antibacterial enzymes that help keep harmful bacteria from developing.

The dog's only sweat glands are on its feet, and function mostly as scent-marking tools rather than a cooling system. Whenever a dog feels too warm, it simply lolls its massive wet tongue out of its mouth, and increases respiration. Air is drawn over the tongue and passed out again, taking with it moisture; panting reduces body heat by evaporation.

Touch

The dog is a social creature that thrives on touching and being touched. A dog's skin is very sensitive to both pain and pleasure. Little dogs snuggle willingly into our laps, and big dogs push as much of their heads and shoulders into our arms as possible, craving their loved one's touch.

The epidermis, the elastic dermis, and the connective tissue of the subcutis compose the three layers of skin that protect the dog from injury, infection, dehydration, and extremes of temperature. Dog skin is much thinner than human skin; their feet can be badly injured by navigating hot asphalt, grit, or stubble. Dogs are susceptible to both sunburn and frostbite, and excessive heat or cold can be fatal.

Extremely sensitive, feathery muscles are dispersed beneath the skin, making each hair a responsive antenna; the most delicate touch brings a dog to attention. Outer guard hairs are exceptionally sensitive, while tactile whiskers (*vibrissae*) are the most sensitive of all and serve to protect the dog's face; grazing the whiskers makes the dog flinch and blink.

Vision

Dogs generally have good eyesight, but it's very different from that of humans. Canine eyes are situated near the front of the face, and relatively far apart, which allows a wide field of vision. The range of vision varies slightly between flat-faced and narrow-headed breeds, but a typical dog's total field of vision is 250 degrees (a human's is 180 degrees).

A DOG'S LIFE

The inner corner of the eye has a "third eyelid" or haw (nictating membrane). The haw acts like a windshield wiper and can cross from one corner of the eye to the other to clean, lubricate, and protect. Some dogs have an obvious haw, while it's almost invisible in others.

The conspicuous colored portion of the eye, called the iris, is a muscular diaphragm that opens and closes the pupil (black portion of the eye) to control the passage of light. Both the pupil and the iris are protected by a thick, transparent cornea. Behind the pupil is the lens, the actual focusing equipment of the eye; on the inside wall at the back of the eyeball is the "movie screen," or retina. The retina contains receptors that respond to light (rods) and color (cones).

The iris expands and contracts depending on the amount and intensity of the available light. The dog sees when light passes through the pupil and is focused by the lens onto the retina. There, rods and cones send signals through the optic nerve to the brain, which translates the data into pictures and tells the dog what it sees.

Dogs lack a fovea, a small rodless area of the retina that provides detail vision in humans. A dog may not recognize a fast-approaching object, and indeed, must back up to see anything that's too close. The dog's binocular field of vision is less than half the width of a person's, so dogs don't judge distance very well.

Instead, dogs rely on movement. A motionless object 300 yards (270m) away is virtually invisible, but at a distance of a mile (1.6km), the dog can see and respond to strong hand signals. Dogs have more light-sensitive cells than man, so their night vision is much better than ours.

- Left: Eye color can range from dark brown/black to very light yellow, blue, or gray.

The ghostly glow of canine eyes at night is caused by a layer of light-reflecting cells behind the retina. This image-intensifying mechanism, called the tapetum lucidum, *acts like a mirror and reflects light back through the retina. Escaping light results in the eerie radiance.*

It used to be thought that dogs only saw in shades of black and white. A large number of rods in the eyes gives dogs an advantage during the monochromatic twilight, but dogs do have cones, and therefore are able to see some degree of color. The eye expert Gordon Walls once said, "The richest of spectral lights could at best appear only as delicate pastel tints of uncertain identity." However, studies have shown that dogs can see reds and blues, and with more difficulty, can distinguish oranges and yellows. To dogs, color just isn't very important. Even so, it's nice to think that our dogs at least have the potential to share our human love of color.

According to a study, about 48 percent of dogs have normal vision, and 52 percent are nearsighted. Dogs with protruding eyes, like Pugs, are more commonly nearsighted than others.

IT'S A DOG'S LIFE

Countless songs celebrate dogs: "Old Dog Tray," "How Much Is That Doggy In The Window," Elvis Presley's "Old Shep" and "You Ain't Nothin' But A Hound Dog" were all howling successes. Some dogs are musicians in their own right; the barking rendition of "Jingle Bells" never fails to make holiday shoppers cringe, but the Paul Winter Consort's breathtaking duet of howling wolves and a saxophone is truly inspirational.

Do dogs appreciate music? Exceptional hearing certainly gives them the potential. Lady, my parents' Sheltie, loved music, and invariably curled up beneath the piano whenever someone played, risking her nose being tromped each time the pedal was pressed. Her Sheltie successor, Pickles, enjoys piano just as much, and likes singing as long as the range is moderate. Pickles telegraphs opinions by tipping her dainty nose to the ceiling and energetically yodeling distaste. Everyone's a critic.

- Right: A dog's hearing and scenting abilities reveal exactly where other animals may be hiding.

Sound Sense

The dog's sense of hearing is extraordinary, and is a valuable aid to humans. Whether floppy, erect, hairy, or bald, the dog's external ears (pinna) are very mobile and can swivel as much as 180 degrees to capture sound. The pinna collect, direct, and reflect air vibrations into the auditory canal, where they strike the tympanic membrane, also called the ear drum. Sound waves set the membranes into sympathetic vibration, amplified by a chain of three bones, the auditory ossicles. The ossicles pass vibrations on to the cochlea, fluid-filled tubes that translate the vibration into nerve impulses. The nerve impulses are conducted by the auditory nerve to the brain, where they are interpreted as sound.

Dogs hear approximately the same low pitches as we do, but their higher range is much better than ours. Human ears can perceive about 20,000 cycles per second; tests indicate that dogs are able to hear waves of frequency as high as 100,000 per second. Dogs can invariably hear the difference between an opening cupboard door that holds doggy shampoo and one that contains puppy crunchies. Even Charlie Brown observed that Snoopy can hear the "munch" of a marshmallow—just like a real dog.

Scent Sense

A dog's "nose print" is as distinctive and individual as a human fingerprint.

Humans take scent for granted. We enjoy the fragrance of cologne and relish the smell of a barbecue, grimace with distaste at the scent of a skunk, and choke on smokey car exhaust. Humans deodorize garbage-can liners, sprinkle carpet powders, and use scented vacuum

A DOG'S LIFE
68

Legend holds that dogs have wet, cold noses from using them to plug holes in Noah's ark. bags; we buy perfumed cleaners and "all natural" sprays for scenting our homes, ourselves, and even our pets. If a smell isn't "pleasant," we cover it up.

Dogs, on the other hand, were born to smell and be smelled. Dogs depend on their awesome olfactory ability for identification, social interaction, and communication; scenting is more important than vision or hearing.

The dog's olfactory sense is useful to humans; dogs have scented out everything from edible fungi, such as truffles, to explosives, drugs, and escaped convicts. All dogs are able to smell a single drop of blood mixed in 5 quarts (4.7l) of water, and some specialist "scenting" dogs are even more adept. Bloodhounds can track a four-day-old trail for up to 100 miles (160km).

The dog's nose is normally cool and moist, which helps retain and assimilate pheromones (scent particles) riding on the air. The nose is composed of the external nares (nostrils) and a nasal cavity divided by a partition into two passages (one for each nostril) that run the entire length of the muzzle. The partition is formed from a massive "scroll-bone" encased in thick, spongy mucous membranes rich in blood vessels, ethmoidal cells, or scent cells, and nerve endings. The nerve endings transmit the most minute olfactory impression directly to the brain.

In humans, the actual scent mechanism contains 5 to 20 million scent cells. In the dog (a German Shepherd, for instance), there are about 200 million ethmoidal cells. Smaller dogs have fewer "scent cells" than larger dogs, but even so, a Dachshund has 125 million such cells.

Dogs have a second scent-detecting organ called the vomeronasal organ (Jacobson's organ) in the roof of the mouth behind the front teeth. Pheromones are transferred to the organ when the dog touches its tongue to the roof of its mouth after licking a scent. A dog will typically puff out its cheeks or chatter its teeth.

The dog's scenting ability depends on what it is smelling. Some smells probably don't mean anything to the dog, but for certain chemicals the dog's ability is phenomenal. The dog's sense of smell is at least a million times better than a person's. To the dog, sniffing is the next best thing to heaven.

- Above: The lovable Chinese Shar-Pei's distinctive looks were developed for defense. The tail is curled to prevent it ever being "tucked" in submission; wrinkles allow it to simply "turn" inside loose skin for counterattack; and prickly fur "feels" bad to a biting dog's mouth.

IT'S A DOG'S LIFE

Educate your dogs, don't just train them.

—Carl "Papa" Spitz Sr., trainer of Toto for the Wizard of Oz *and other films.*

DOG BEHAVIOR

Dogs are extremely intelligent; in fact, they're so smart they often train their owners instead of the other way around. You provide for and protect your dog, but that's not enough to keep it healthy and happy. Dogs are social creatures that need structure and guidance. Dogs naturally challenge authority, so a position of command must be established early and routinely reinforced. By all means be your dog's friend; but be sure you are also the "pack leader."

Rules of the House

Dog training is the subject of numerous excellent and detailed reference guides, which any new dog owner should be sure to consult, but there are some basic guidelines to understand. Among these, perhaps the most important is that puppies must be taught very early the meaning of a solid, authoritative "No!" This is often all that's necessary to correct poor behavior. Talk to your dog. Dogs have the ability to learn a huge vocabulary, and the more your puppy understands, the fewer misunderstandings and behavioral problems there will be.

Remember that dogs are very sensitive to nuances of sound, and often react more to emotion and body language than specific words. Be sure your vocal tone and facial expression reflect what you mean; shaming your pet while you laugh is pointless, for sending mixed signals will only confuse the animal.

Learning should be an enjoyable process for both you and your pet. Most dogs idolize their human owner and want to please, but dwelling on negatives will teach your dog that more attention is forthcoming for doing something wrong. Remember, too, that discouragement can make the dog give up. Always end a session on an up note—pick something you know your dog can do. Then reward successful behavior with a play session.

If your dog doesn't understand your instruction, it's not fair and can even be detrimental to reprimand. Praise enthusiastically when your pet does something right—when it comes on command or chews the rawhide toy instead of your high heels. Remember that consistency is key.

Never give a command you don't intend to enforce. When you give in, the dog wins a victory. With enough victories, your pet will rightfully assume that it is the leader of the pack, not you, and will start making decisions you won't like. You have to stay Top Dog.

• Above: The "stay" command can be given verbally or as a hand signal.

A DOG'S LIFE
70

Never allow your puppy to get away with growling or snapping at you. As an adult, such a dog could become dangerous. It would then require qualified and expensive professional help to adequately address the problem.

Firm verbal chastisement (never shout) is effective alone or in combination with other forms of reprimand; with very sensitive dogs, a disappointed "Shame on you!" may suffice. Abrupt noises startle and interrupt poor behavior. A coffee can filled with loose change rattled loudly at appropriate times, along with a verbal reprimand, often works wonders. Scruff shaking simulates the discipline meted out by a mother dog and is effective for hard cases; firmly grasp the loose skin on the back of the neck and shake hard (don't lift the dog from the floor). This will clarify who is pack leader. Corporeal punishment is ineffective and often damages the dog's personality. Never slap or hit your dog; it will learn to associate your hands with punishment.

Effective Correction and Rewards

Use reprimands only during or immediately following poor behavior. Dogs have short memories when it comes to infractions, and punishing after the fact won't correct the behavior; no dog will understand the shoe chewed three hours ago has anything to do with the here and now. Chasing after the dog as you scold will either make it fear you or believe you're playing a game.

Teach your dog to allow things to be taken from its mouth, so you can safely remove hazardous food or objects if necessary.

Use food sparingly as a reward; although bribes may bring fast results, many dogs come to expect a tidbit and refuse to perform without one. Most dogs react just as well to verbal praise; your encouragement and attention should be reward enough. Please consider obedience training for your dog. Humane organizations have listings for professional trainers and obedience clubs in your area. Hint: it works better if you train with your dog!

Finicky Eaters

Smart dogs often buffalo their owners into offering unhealthy meals, but most bad eating habits can be reversed by disciplining ourselves, rather than our pets. A poor appetite may indicate health problems, but once this is ruled out, a strict regimen will correct the habit. Your veterinarian can recommend a good brand of food, the proper feeding schedule, and the right amount for your pet's size, age, and energy needs.

Feeding should take place at the same time each day, with the food offered at fifteen-minute intervals. If your dog begs for something else, sternly say, "No!," and take it to its bowl. Praise the dog when it eats what is offered, but once time has expired, pick up the food whether eaten or not. Don't feed again until the next scheduled meal.

If used to getting its own way, your dog will probably resist your effort. Don't be surprised if your pet refuses the first meal, or even two or three meals in order to test your willpower. Be strong; when a dog gets hungry

Hard foods keep teeth cleaner and healthier than soft and moist foods. Table scraps will often upset a dog's digestion, promote eating disorders, and cause dental problems.

• Above: A Chocolate Labrador Retriever lounging in the summer grass.

IT'S A DOG'S LIFE

Chocolate contains theobromine, a chemical that is toxic to dogs.

enough, it'll eat what you know is best, not what it wants. Remember, a thinner dog will live a longer, healthier life. Soon your dog will learn to eat what is offered before it is removed—and you'll be able to tell when it might really be ill as opposed to gold-bricking for handouts.

Jumping on People

A small dog jumping up on people may be cute or simply annoying, but large dogs can cause injury. Be consistent; your dog won't understand why it's okay to jump on you, but not other people. Pushing a playful dog away (even with your knee) invites further play and greatly excites the dog. Stepping on the dog's toes

The nasty, yet quite common habit of eating animal droppings is called coprophagia. Your veterinarian can supply capsules that give the feces a bad taste to deter such practices.

associates the infliction of pain with an affectionate bid for attention. Use your coffee can noise-maker, or sharply tug down on the dog's training collar while commanding "Off!" to deter the behavior. Insist the dog sit when you arrive home, and reward good behavior.

Mounting Inappropriately

In an unaltered male dog, a level of sexual frustration can build until he attempts to mate with anything that doesn't move: the table, a chair, your leg. Dogs think that humans are members of the same species and grab legs because they are easy to clasp. Neutering relieves you both of the physical and emotional turmoil.

• Right: Great friendships and devotion grow from mutual respect.

A DOG'S LIFE

Digging

Many dogs, particularly terriers, enjoy digging. Provide the excavator with a "digging place" where it can tunnel to its heart's content. Fence off-limits areas, or supervise constantly and chastise for inappropriate digging. Areas that you want to protect can be booby-trapped with the dog's buried feces as a most effective deterrent.

Do You Speak Dog?

Dog dialogue is not easy to master; most dog communication is accomplished using body signals and smells. Although we aren't equipped to interpret the finer points, most dog lovers understand a lot more than they think.

A direct stare and snarl are warnings to keep your distance. Running from a dog or making any quick motions stimulates a dog's chase and attack instincts. When threatened by a strange dog, hold your ground, or back up very slowly with a smooth motion.

Aggression within limits is natural. Posturing establishes who is Top Dog, and prevents actual fights. Threatening dogs typically fix opponents with intimidating stares, snarl to reveal teeth, and hold their ears erect. The head is high, movement is stiff, and fur along the back stands on end. Threatening dogs may lift a leg and urinate, then scratch the ground while bristling and growling.

Usually such a display is sufficient to determine dominance, and one dog will back down; however, some encounters escalate to attack. An attacking dog plasters its ears against the side of its head, probably to protect them. During intense threat or attack, the head may lower and neck extend as the dog "points" its adversary.

Submissive body language is the reverse of aggressive displays. Aggressive dogs try to look bigger by fluffing out their fur and standing on their toes; the submissive pooch wants to appear smaller. Just as aggressive displays encourage distance, submissive displays invite proximity.

Adult dogs have strong inhibitions about attacking puppies; therefore, subordinate adult dogs act like puppies to avoid being attacked. When threatened, a submissive dog crouches, rolls onto its back, exposes the genitals, and perhaps even urinates in the ultimate show of submission. To approach a dominant figure, the dog crouches to appear "puppy-size," then crawls forward and reaches up to lick and nuzzle the face the same way puppies beg food from adults.

Any dog, no matter the breed, has the potential to be dangerous; a 1982 study of fatal dog attacks included such breeds as Yorkshire Terriers and Dachshunds.

• Below: Consistency and patience will teach puppies your rules.

IT'S A DOG'S LIFE

Some dogs urinate when verbally corrected by owners, and others urinate from excitement when the owner returns home. Punishing a show of submission makes it worse; most puppies will outgrow it. Adult dogs that persist in submissive urination often learn to control themselves if their owner ignores them the first five to ten minutes after returning home.

Other signs of submission include avoiding eye contact in an exaggerated fashion; ears flattening against the head; tucking the tail or wagging in a low position; tongue flicking out to indicate a desire to lick; and raising or offering a forepaw, a prologue to rolling over.

Ambivalent signals occur when a dog is in a state of conflicting emotion. Maybe it is afraid yet aggressive, or curious and submissive at the same time. The fear-biter may show elements of aggression along with fear; hackles may be raised, but tail tucked tight, with an aggressive facial expression.

Barking

The fearless dog attacks in silence. A snarl indicates slight fear. Growling is a sign of deeper fear, and barks changing to or mixed with growls indicate the dog is probably more fearful than aggressive. The timid dog flees in silence.

The phonation that produces the dog's voice varies depending on size and shape of its vocal chords and muzzle, as well as speed and power of lung capacity. The dogs' vocal repertory is tied to body movement and generally indicates its emotional state.

Whining is a distress call aimed at humans; the pleading sound often occurs when a dog is left alone or is punished. The bark is a canine alert that warns the "pack" of anything unusual, like the arrival of a friend or stranger, and is not necessarily a sign of aggression.

- Above, right: All dogs can howl, but polar-type breeds may indulge most often, a trait they have in common with wolf cousins.

Excessive barking is aggravating, and is a dominant act on the part of the dog. Breeds with a watchdog background may be more prone to overindulge. Allow and even praise initial barking; the dog has alerted the pack (you), so acknowledge a job well done. Continued barking should be halted with an appropriate command, such as "Enough," or "Quiet." Don't yell; yelling may be perceived as a "barking contest," and your dog will happily join the competition.

Howls basically mean, "I am here; please join me," and in the wild serve to call the pack together. If isolated, some dogs howl from loneliness. In musical families, the singing or playing of instruments often prompts dogs to join in what they perceive to be a friendly howl-along.

A DOG'S LIFE

Tail of the Dog

A wagging tail conveys joy. Basically, the tail is held high by confident dogs, and low or tucked by shy or insecure canines. In submissive dogs, wags are loose and wide, while aggressive dogs wag in short arcs. The highly held tail allows anal sniffing and scent identification; the tucked tail cuts off this avenue of exploration, just like a shy human hiding the face.

Sniffing

When dogs meet, they first smell each other's faces, then direct their attention to each other's anal area. Wagging with the tail held high spreads the anal gland scent on the air. Anal glands are two pea-size organs located on each side of the rectum that add a strong-smelling scent to feces and give each dog its individual scent identity. Dragging the rump, or "scooting," is usually a means of seeking relief from impacted anal glands, which occur more commonly in small dogs.

Rolling

At puberty, a male dog will start cocking its leg against different objects to spray urine. This behavior is called marking. What do the scent marks mean? Dog urine contains sexual information, allows individual identification, and may indicate "occupied" territory. Leg-cocking enables the scent to be placed at doggy nose level; an upright object (such as a fire hydrant) may act as a visual signpost, telling other dogs where to sniff. Dogs become enraptured reading the scented "business cards" left by others, then obliterate the marks with their own.

In laboratory settings, dogs go into a kind of "scent ecstasy" and roll on almost any strong odor, including lemon rind, tobacco, and perfume. Frequently, dogs roll in more noxious aromas — the equivalent of dabbing on doggy perfume. To your dog, rotten fish or ripe cowpats may be the essence of high fashion.

Dogs scratch the ground after elimination to leave visual and scent markings from sweat glands between the toes.

• Left: Dogs also roll to scratch that hard-to-reach itch.

IT'S A DOG'S LIFE

REPRODUCTION

A Greyhound named "Timmy" of London, England, sired more than 3,024 puppies in an eight-year period.

Dogs are able to sire puppies by ten months, and some bitches experience their first heat (estrus) as early as six months. Estrus usually occurs about every six to eight months, and generally lasts twenty-one days. Proestrus is the onset of the heat cycle, lasts six to nine days, and is indicated by a dark bloody discharge and swelling of the vulva. Standing heat occurs during ovulation, and is the receptive phase during which the discharge lightens from dark red to a faint pinkish color. Standing heat lasts about six to twelve days, and ends when the bitch refuses the male. Most dogs are bred between day ten and day fourteen of estrus.

During ovulation, eggs that are shed must mature for seventy-two hours before they can be fertilized by sperm; however, the dog's sperm is able to survive up to seven days in the uterus.

- Above: Samoyed puppies in the sled they'll someday pull. All puppies are curious and anxious to learn.

In arranged breedings, the bitch is sent to the male dog. He makes his own explorations, sniffing and posturing, while the female becomes coy and flirtatious; she'll flag and raise her tail to the side, and present her vulva to him when she's ready. The stud dog mounts the female, clasps her with his forelegs, and inserts his penis. At full penetration, he stops thrusting forward, and treads up and down with his hind paws.

When a knot at the base of the penis (bulbus glandis) becomes swollen, it's held firmly by the muscles of the vagina, causing the mating dogs to become "tied" together. The swelling induces ejaculation, which occurs in three stages; an initial clear spermless fluid is followed by a second ejaculation containing sperm, and then a final third ejaculation of prostatic fluid propels the sperm into the uterus. The prolonged tie seems to be a way of ensuring enough time for the process to be complete. The tie lasts three to forty minutes and sometimes longer; duration has no effect on success of mating or the number of resulting puppies.

Gestation is usually about sixty-three days. A veterinarian can determine pregnancy by palpation at about twenty-six days of gestation, but later than that the uterus becomes filled with fluid and the "puppy bumps" are no longer discernible. If breeding has been successful, the first clear sign will be an enlarging and darkening of the nipples at about forty days of gestation.

A few days before the birth, the mother-to-be will start looking for a good place to bear her puppies and may go about in a flurry of activity, rummaging in closets or rearranging her bedding. Provide her with a special, private place to give birth. This may prevent her from whelping on your bedspread. She should be used to sleeping in the whelping box by the time her puppies are due.

A DOG'S LIFE

Litter size varies depending on breed, but the average is five puppies. An American Foxhound named Lena bore a record litter of twenty-three puppies in 1945.

About eight to twelve hours before whelping, the expectant dog's temperature will abruptly drop about two degrees (1° C). The first stage of labor begins with rapid panting, anxiousness, straining, and possibly vomiting. Each puppy will be encased in a bag of fluid that helps lubricate the passage; if the bag is ruptured during labor, a straw-colored fluid will be passed, and should be shortly followed by a puppy. The placenta, or afterbirth, follows each birth; a retained placenta can cause problems, so be alert. Puppies are normally born fifteen minutes to two hours apart.

If a puppy is very cold and weak, dunk it up to its neck in a bowl of 101°F (38°C) water (the average puppy body temperature) for two to three minutes, then stroke and massage until it becomes more active, then dry with warm towels. If the puppy is too weak to breathe, squeeze the chest gently from side to side and back to front; mouth-to-nose respiration (very gentle breaths!) may stimulate breathing. Have a veterinarian check on the new mother and her puppies the day after delivery.

When to Get Help

During the Birth: If bearing down produces no puppies after two hours; if a dark green or bloody discharge is passed before the first puppy is born (after the first birth this discharge is normal); if clear yellow (amniotic) fluid appears and a puppy isn't delivered within thirty minutes; if the mother is in extreme pain; if she is trembling, shivering, or collapses; or if labor stops, but she is still carrying puppies.

After the Birth: If there is a heavy, dark, bloody greenish or tomato-souplike discharge accompanied by fever; if the mother is lethargic; if normal eating doesn't resume in twelve hours; if she is abnormally restless, and exhibits stiff-legged jerky pacing with rapid respiration; or if she shows no interest in her puppies.

© Alice Garik

• Left: Dominance is determined shortly after birth, as puppies compete for food and position in the litter.

IT'S A DOG'S LIFE

Orphan puppies must be fed three to four times daily (the amount depends on the puppy's weight), and during the first three weeks must be stimulated to eliminate. After each feeding, gently massage the anal area with cotton dipped in warm water.

- Above, right: A puppy's facial expressions and personality develop early.

PUPPY DEVELOPMENT

As each puppy is born, the bitch breaks the membrane and licks them to stimulate breathing and circulation. She shreds the cord, and often eats the afterbirth. Puppies immediately seek a breast; the first milk (colostrum) contains important antibodies and nutrients.

If the mother doesn't open the sack, do it yourself, and rub the baby vigorously with warm towels to stimulate breathing. Tie the cord and cut about 2 inches (5cm) from the abdomen, then disinfect the cut end with iodine. Use a bulb syringe to clear fluid from the mouth; or, hold the puppy securely and fling it head-down between your legs toward the floor, so centrifugal force clears the passages.

A newborn's eyes and ears are sealed, but its sense of smell is already well developed. Puppies use their heads and faces as sensors to find warm, soft surfaces. Each puppy competes with its littermates for the best nipple. The puppies spend about 10 percent of the time eating, and the rest sleeping together in a pile.

A puppy's ability to regulate its own body temperature isn't well developed until two to three weeks of age. At birth, its temperature ranges from 92° to 97°F (33° to 36°C), but close body contact with its mother keeps temperature 96° to 100°F (35° to 38°C).

Puppies' eyes and ears open at ten to sixteen days. Crawling begins at birth, and wobbly standing occurs at about fifteen days. By three weeks, puppies are walking and getting into all kinds of trouble; but the accompanying tail wagging and barking that begin at this age keeps you smiling through each trespass.

Twenty-eight milk teeth erupt between three and five weeks of age; large breed dogs teethe earlier than toy breeds. The mother's milk starts to diminish at about the same time, and she begins to wean her puppies in earnest; it generally takes a week for the puppies to get the message. At this age, puppies naturally imitate her, and can be trained to drink from a bowl.

Aside from just plain being fun, play helps develop motor and social skills and prepares puppies for life. At the age of three weeks, puppies are chewing each other's ears and licking and pawing at their mother's and each other's faces. This is an important learning experience that teaches the puppy just how hard it can bite (or be bitten) without causing pain. It soon discovers how to inhibit the bite.

Proper socialization is extremely important. It's a good idea to expose puppies to a variety of situations: invite guests to handle and play with them, allow your other (healthy) dogs and cats to interact with them. A professional Cocker Spaniel breeder for over twenty years, Marion Hunt crate-trains puppies at five weeks by

A DOG'S LIFE

letting them play in the dog crate together, so the crate becomes a "happy place." Poorly socialized puppies grow fearful of strange situations and may become either extremely shy or aggressive biters.

At about four to five weeks, puppies chase each other and grab the scruff of necks. They learn and perfect the prey-shaking head movements. Through pounce and snap, growl and snarl, bared fang and offered tummy, they learn to show submission, aggression, and invitation to play. By five weeks, unique facial expressions evolve as puppies learn to manipulate ears and lips, and display teeth. An extensive vocal repertoire develops; puppies become proficient at barks, snarls, yipes, and whines, each carrying important meaning.

Let's Play

By five weeks, puppies often carry things around. They play tug-of-war and may even guard a toy or piece of food. At this age, they begin to urinate and defecate in one designated area some distance from their beds. Both male and female puppies squat to urinate; male "leg-cocking" begins at eight or nine months. By six weeks, the puppy has learned its lessons and knows all the behavior patterns of the adult.

The Healthy Puppy

By eight weeks of age, a puppy is ready to leave its mother and go to a new home. When selecting a puppy, always choose a healthy animal; sick puppies start life with several strikes against them. The eyes and nose

When lifting your puppy, cup its bottom with one hand and its chest (behind the forelegs) with the other. Lift adults with the same care, supporting both chest and hindquarters. Never lift a dog by its front legs.

should be free of discharge; the nose should be cool and moist, the gums pink; the inside of ears ought to look and smell clean; the coat must be bright and shiny, and skin should be free of scabs, scales, redness, or bald spots; the anal area must be free of diarrhea or discharge; and male puppies ought to have both testicles visible. Puppies should be happy, alert, very active, and playful. Shrinking violets and aggressive cases haven't been properly socialized, and both extremes cause problems. The perfect puppy is healthy, follows you with its tail held high, is active, thrives on petting, may struggle when initially held but then relaxes and accepts being picked up.

Dogs play to some extent through their entire adulthood. In order to make clear that the playful chasing or fleeing is not "real," dogs use elaborate signals. The most obvious invitation to play is the canine "bow," when the rear end is stuck high in the air while the forequarters are lowered so the chest nearly touches the ground. Dogs also display a grinning "play face" as well as nudge with their noses, paw, and offer an object to induce a game of "keep away." Sometimes they display exaggerated jumping and twirling, running and zig-zagging. Dominant dogs may use a reassurance display; they flop on their backs and pretend to be submissive, so the other dog feels brave enough for play to begin.

● Above: A frolicsome German Shepherd puppy playing peek-a-boo.

IT'S A DOG'S LIFE

To playful puppies, everything is a toy to be bitten, chewed, and shaken. Chewing also helps a puppy's adult teeth break through, which happens at above four months. In the wild, adult wolf-pack members bring prey to the den for puppies to practice killing, and it's natural for a puppy to treat anything the "pack leader" leaves laying around as fair game.

• Small puppies are notorious chewers, and this beagle is living up to that reputation.

A Gnawing Habit

Teething puppies are notorious chewers. Sometimes older dogs retain the habit as well. Dogs need to chew to maintain oral hygiene, and chewing also has a calming effect. Repellants such as Chew Guard protect treated objects from an ardent chewer, but limiting opportunities to chew will go a long way toward changing problem behavior.

Don't give old shoes, socks, children's toys, or other hand-me-downs to your pet. It won't know the difference between an old shoe and your brand new loafers. When the puppy tries to play tug-of-war with any of your things, don't permit it for a second. Although fun, such contests encourage your dog to bite down and hang on; your dog should instead release objects when you grasp them. Reprimand the puppy and immediately substitute a "legal" toy. Ideal toys include nylon or rawhide bones that indulge the dog's urge to chew.

Never *give your dog real bones or allow sticks or rocks as chewing toys. They may damage teeth and cause deadly obstructions or punctures if swallowed.*

Older dogs that chew inappropriately may be bored or lonely; make sure acceptable chew toys are available. Try to determine what's causing the chewing—is the dog alone much of the time? Does it get enough exercise? When you've identified the problem, you can try to correct it. Some dog psychologists recommend getting your pet a pet—if not another dog, then a fish, turtle, hamster, or even a parakeet may divert a chewer for hours. (Keep in mind the new pet will need attention from you, too!)

The Second Pet

Introduce new dogs (or cats) on "neutral" territory that neither pet feels impelled to defend. Allow them to get acquainted (on leash). Have a friend bring the new pet to your home, so you aren't blamed for the intrusion. It's natural for the old-timer to growl and assert dominance, but excessive roughness shouldn't be tolerated. Be sure to give the older pet plenty of attention, so it doesn't feel displaced.

Puppy Puddles and Plops

Dog lovers dread the unpleasant "surprises" that are inevitably left scattered about the house by a new puppy. Unless you plan to use paper-training for life, house-training your puppy to use an outside area for elimination without the intermediate paper chase is quicker and more effective. A cardboard box (or crate) is an inexpensive teaching tool that works.

Dogs avoid messing their bed, so confine the puppy to a space only large enough for bedding and a small bowl of water. Use a box or crate: even the kitchen or laundry room is a huge space to a tiny puppy, and it will simply eliminate in one corner and sleep in the other. Anticipate the dog's internal clock (after naps, meals, and playtime) and always take it to the same place so it will identify that area as the appropriate place. When a mistake happens, scold only if you catch the puppy in

A DOG'S LIFE

the act, then immediately remove the puppy to the designated area. Praise enthusiastically whenever your puppy relieves itself in the right place.

Many local governments have enacted "pooper-scooper laws" that enforce good manners among dog owners. Generally, these laws require dog owners to immediately and sanitarily dispose of droppings deposited anywhere except on their own property.

Box the puppy whenever it's not under direct supervision. That means if you leave the room or get a phone call, put the puppy in a box. This is not cruel, although many puppies will cry to convince you otherwise. Confinement teaches a painless, effective, and quick lesson. The alternative is living with adult-size puddles and plops, which are unthinkable, particularly if you've chosen a St. Bernard. Confinement teaches a puppy to let you know when it needs to go out, in order to avoid messing in its bed. Discontinue crating only when the puppy consistently warns you of its needs. Try the box for at least a week; it may take longer, but many puppies learn within the first several days.

Diet can help reduce both the bulk and odor of solid wastes. Ask your veterinarian to recommend an appropriate and healthy brand of dog food.

Dogs "go" in the wrong places for any number of reasons; they may be reacting to changes in your home—a new baby, marriage, divorce, or the addition of a new pet or loss of an old pet. Insufficient training may be at fault, or the dog may be using bodily functions to challenge authority and exhibit displeasure. Most importantly, dogs break training when they're sick. Whenever an accident occurs, be sure you know why, so you can act appropriately to prevent recurrence.

A one-year-old dog is physiologically equal to a thirteen-year old-child, and a two-year-old dog is like a twenty-year-old adult. From age three on, each year is equivalent to about five of ours.

Once the dog starts using a corner of the room, it's a hard habit to break. Clean "accidents" with a commercial odor neutralizer such as Nature's Miracle to discourage a repeat performance. Older dogs that habitually leave little presents around the house will also respond to confinement; it may take longer to break them of the habit, but the results will be well worth the effort. The key to a future free of annoyance is today's patience and consistency. Your entire family, (and your carpet) will love you for it.

● Below: Puppies mature much faster than human infants, but "potty training" is a challenge for both.

IT'S A DOG'S LIFE

81

Nobody's Dog

Today, I found Nobody's Dog. Her ribs were beginning to show through a once shiny black coat. At first, she tucked her tail tightly and ran, then, ever hopeful, returned with a tentative wag.

I bet she was cute as a puppy. Somebody picked her out special, took her home, and made her believe she would always be loved; but some humans change their minds and their loves as often as dirty socks. Even so, the betrayed black dog is still loving them, futilely waiting for them to come back for her. She had a name once, and now she can't understand, for you see, a dog's love never dies.

Today, I found Nobody's Dog, one of millions abandoned each year by owners that take the coward's way out. They won't see her slowly starve or freeze to death, be hit by a car, or live at the mercy of strangers as she begs for a scrap of attention.

Today, the Shelter rescued Nobody's Dog. There, she'll be fed, she'll be loved, and hopefully she'll be claimed by a more fitting, deserving human. If not, she'll go to an even better place, one where dogs are always loved and are never thrown away on a cruel whim. But she still yearns to be Somebody's Dog once more.

DOGS AND PEOPLE

Canine Responsibility

Every second, another puppy is born; each minute, fifty-six new furry faces yipe and cry; every hour, more than 3,000 puppies, a staggering 80,600 daily, are added to the horrendous total. Twenty-four million healthy, loving dogs and cats are euthanized every year, and countless more are abandoned because there just aren't enough good homes to go around.

According to the United Nations, there are approximately 135 million pet dogs in the world; 54.5 million are kept in the United States alone.

No one can deny that a cuddly puppy is adorable, and that a basketful of the wee beasties is the ultimate in fuzzy puppy love. But it's essential that all dog fanciers realize their responsibility to prevent rather than perpetuate puppy births. There is indeed a litter problem, and not just along the highways. Informed dog lovers know the "puppy-lation" explosion isn't a result of love, but of ignorance and mismanagement.

It's a crime against dogdom to breed your dog, male or female. Each litter member that finds a home eliminates a prospective sanctuary for another puppy; in effect, producing puppies actually sentences others to death. There is no valid excuse to allow any dog to roam and breed. Spayed and neutered dogs make better, more affectionate companions; intact dogs often develop behavior and temperament problems.

Neutering males reduces roaming and aggression, and nearly eliminates the chance of prostate cancer. Spaying females frees them of the inconveniences of estrus and

A DOG'S LIFE

Twenty-six percent of all intact female dogs over five years old get mammary cancer. subsequent courting by male dogs. It also prevents uterine and ovarian cancer. In addition, spaying before the first heat cycle reduces the risk of mammary cancer to 0.5 percent.

Reputable fanciers breed only a very few extraordinary dogs, and then only to improve the breed. Cocker Spaniel breeder Marion Hunt has spayed her dogs and suspended breeding. "It's getting very difficult to find good homes," explains Marion, "and the home my puppies go to is more important than anything else." Most professional breeders are strong proponents of altering, and many urge that pet-quality puppies be sterilized when they are placed. Unfortunately, there are many irresponsible people breeding dogs; the "puppy mills" are a vivid example. There are also well-meaning individuals who jump into breeding without adequate preparation or knowledge.

A puppy mill is literally a factory for live merchandise. Typically, adult dogs are housed in tiny wire cages. They are rarely allowed out, but must relieve themselves on the wire floor, and stand and live in the mess. Because of the wire, the dog's feet often become painfully deformed. Health care is poor or nonexistent; adults are kept solely to breed, and females are bred every heat cycle until they wear out, and are then destroyed. Puppies are generally sold in bulk to chain pet stores and are so poorly socialized they make extremely poor pets. Many have infectious diseases or genetic disorders from improper health and breeding standards, and often such puppies die before they reach adulthood. Puppy mills are shops of horror that make their bloody profit by mass-producing damaged, inferior puppies.

Poor Excuses

People offer all kinds of excuses to justify breeding their dogs:

1. "Fixing Prince/Princess will make the dog fat and lazy." *Dogs, like people, get fat by overeating and not exercising enough.*

2. "I hear it matures the dog to have one litter before spaying." *People hear this from self-appointed "experts"; there's no scientific or medical evidence that having a litter is good for your pet.*

3. "I fix the mutts, but King/Queen's a purebred." *Twenty-five percent of all dogs left at shelters are purebreds that no one wanted.*

4. "King's getting old, and I want one of his puppies before he dies." *Genetics is an inexact science; no puppy, not even King's son, will be just like him.*

5. "It's educational for my children to witness the miracle of birth." *Children learn that puppies can be created and discarded as it suits us. (Instead, check with your veterinarian; they often have films available for viewing.) Emphasize the real miracle, which is life; teach your children that preventing the births of some pets saves the lives of others.*

• Above: A Golden Retriever puppy guarding his field of flowers.

IT'S A DOG'S LIFE
83

Puppies can learn more and learn faster from age six weeks to four months than they will after they're six months old.

—Kim Lindemoen, trainer of animal actors

If I can't convince you not to breed your dog, then at least do it in an intelligent and humane fashion. Read books, quiz your veterinarian, and most importantly, study with a reputable breeder who knows firsthand the pitfalls and demands of breeding. Think ahead: competition is fierce; what will you do if the puppies can't be sold? Do you want to risk placing them in less-than-desirable homes, or will you be able to keep them yourself? Please, don't add to the litter of the highways.

One female dog and her offspring can produce, in a six-year period, 67,000 puppies. More than 17 million puppies will be born in the United States this year alone; the RSPCA in Great Britain must destroy 1,000 dogs a day, and the Toronto Humane Society estimates that 350,000 dogs pass through Canadian shelters every year. Eighty percent of the puppies born this year are destined to be surrendered or abandoned.

That's more than 21.5 million puppies, a staggering four out of every litter of five, that will end up as victims of abandonment, starvation and disease, or be humanely euthanized.

That puppy ecstatically licking your face is the lucky fifth. Before you permit the suffering to continue, please listen; the clock's still ticking.

Dog Laws

Assistance dogs are often exempted from requirements imposed on other dogs.

The local animal-control office, health department, or municipal code (available at public libraries) should be able to offer specific information on laws governing dogs in your community.

• Right: Malamute puppy.

A DOG'S LIFE

In most regions, animal-control authorities are sanctioned to seize biting dogs or dogs proven to be incorrigible nuisances; owners have the right to be notified before the dog is seized or destroyed, and given a chance to argue in court that the dog shouldn't be destroyed. You may lose your right to notice if the dog is unlicensed or running at large. Almost all laws require license tags to be on a dog at all times, and most licenses require proof of rabies vaccination; you may need a new license if moving to a new city, county, state, or province. Leash laws require dogs to be on a leash and under human control whenever off of their owner's property. Loose running dogs may be impounded by the animal shelter, and the owner fined. Dogs at pounds are either reclaimed by owners, adopted, sold (usually to research labs), or destroyed. Many facilities can't keep animals longer than three to seven days.

Certainly we mourn our pets, but they grieve for us as well. Greyfriars' Bobby held watch over his master's grave in Edinburgh's historic Greyfriars churchyard for fourteen years, until his own death. Shep mourned twelve years outside the hospital where his beloved master Francis McMahon had died. When Hachiko's master died, all of Japan learned of the faithful Akita that returned to the train station each day at five o'clock to search for his beloved master. The Japanese government erected a statue on the spot where Hachiko kept his ten-year vigil. If there's any justice, all faithful dogs are in death finally reunited with their masters.

Have you made arrangements for someone to care for your dog in the event of your illness or death? Remember: a dog is considered property, and can't inherit. Instead of leaving property or money to your dog, leave any monies necessary for the care of your dog with a guardian named in your will, and specify that the funds be used solely for the dog. Consult a lawyer for specifics.

In many cities, it's become nearly impossible to find decent rental property that will accept even well-mannered dogs. Offer to pay a security deposit; provide written references from previous landlords and obedience schools; suggest a face-to-face meeting with your dog for an evaluation; and agree to abide by equitable limitations (pooper-scooper and leash restrictions). Never sign a lease that retains a "no pets" clause; have such clauses removed or amended to protect you from a landlord's change of heart or a change in apartment ownership.

• Above: Alter your dog to prevent unplanned litters.

IT'S A DOG'S LIFE

• Three dogs on a mountainside near Salt Lake City, Utah.

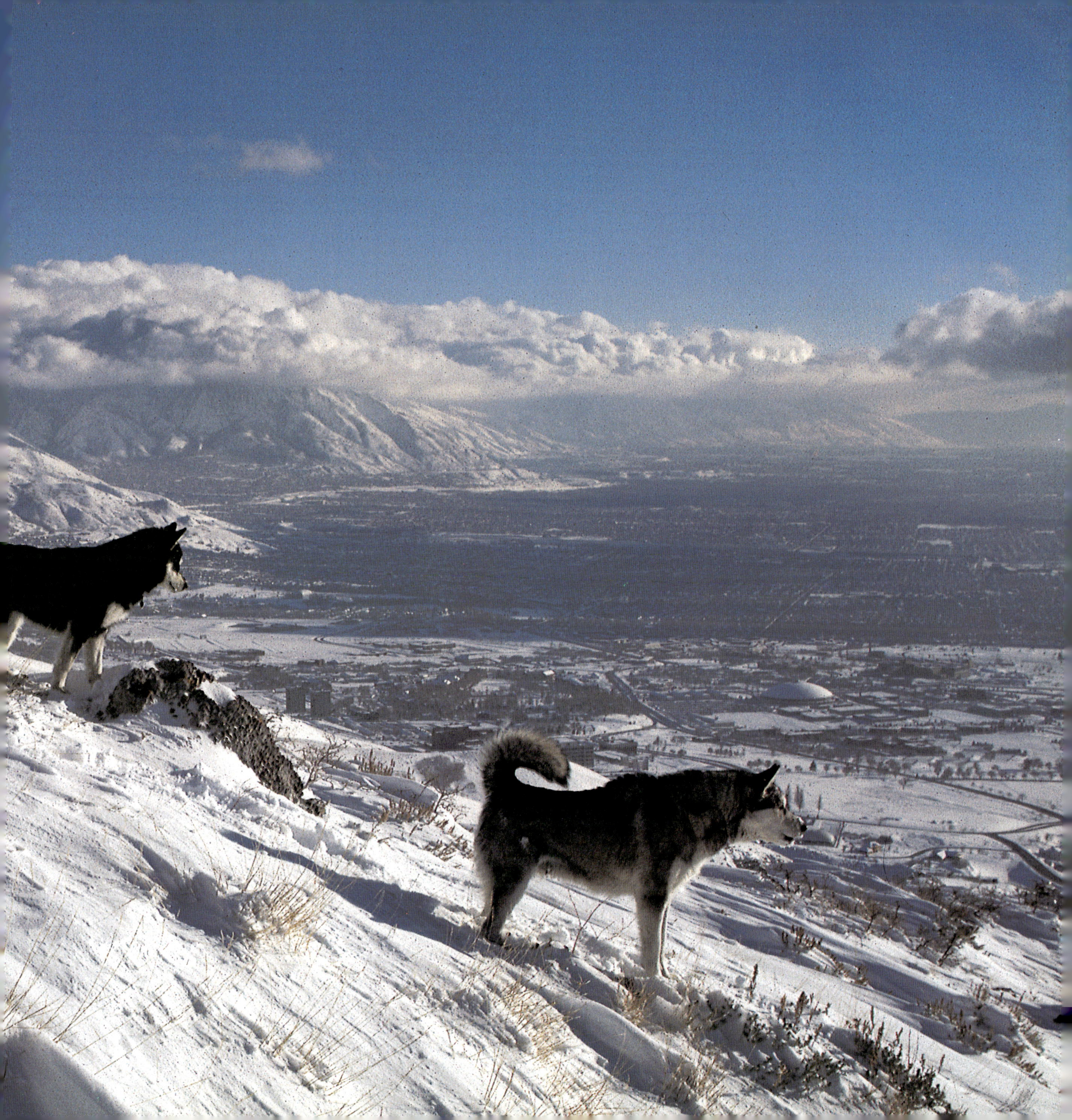

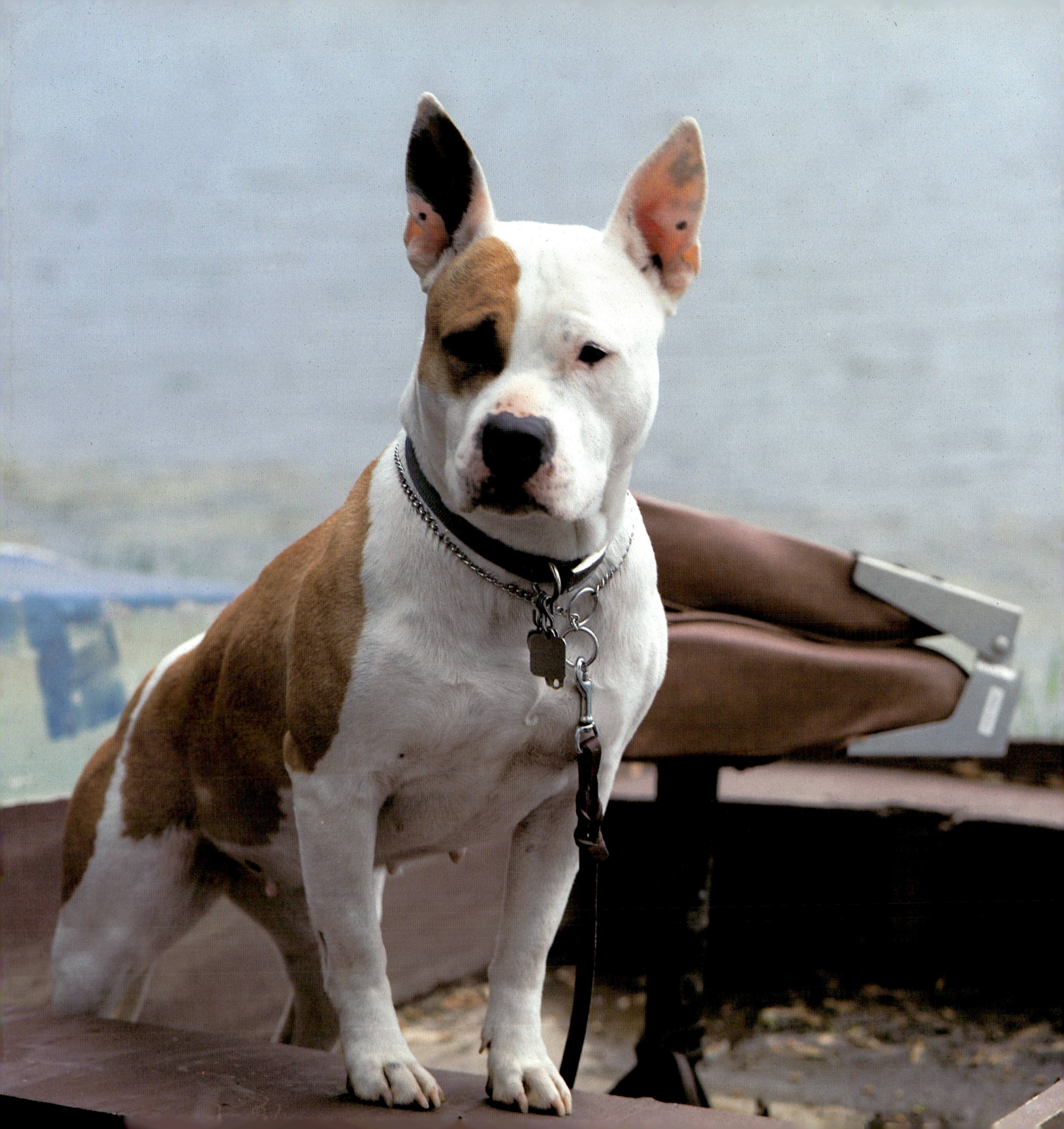

One night in 1888, a small, plain mutt wandered into the Albany, New York, post office. Owney liked to ride trains, and often became restless and snuck on board mail shipments. A tag was attached to his collar that read, "To all who may greet this dog, Owney is his name. He is the pet of 100,000 mail clerks in the United States. Treat him kindly and speed him on his journey, across ocean and land." Owney wandered from Canada to Alaska and Mexico, and even stowed away on a mail ship to Japan; upon his arrival he was honored by the Mikado and received an award from the Emperor. From Japan, Owney traveled to China and beyond. Postal workers all over the world attached medals and tags (1,017 in all) to his collar. Today, Owney can be seen in the Smithsonian Institute in Washington, D.C.

The Traveling Dog

A health certificate with proof of recent vaccinations is required when traveling with your dog to another state, province, or country. Overseas restrictions also apply: permits must be applied for several weeks in advance, and quarantines are often necessary. England requires a six-month quarantine, and Hawaii quarantines all dogs, even guide and service dogs, for 120 days.

Guide, service, and signal dogs fly free in the airline cabin with their owners. Airlines aren't set up to deal with pets; basically, your dog will be treated as luggage, subjected to stuffy or freezing baggage compartments and dangerous or careless handling. If small enough to fit in a carrier under the seat, your dog may qualify as "carry-on" luggage, but many airlines allow only one animal in the cabin per flight, so call ahead.

Traveling by car is generally more convenient and comfortable for your dog, but many hotels and motels won't accept pets. The ASPCA published *Traveling with Your Pet*, and the Gaines Dog Food Company offers a guide to pet-accepting motels called *Touring with Towser*. Both provide helpful tips for planning trips with your dog (for those living outside the United States, contact your local SPCA):

ASPCA
Traveling with Your Pet (enclose $5)
424 East 92nd Street
New York, NY 10128

Gaines Touring with Towser (enclose $1.50)
P.O. Box 5700
Kankakee, IL 60902

Cruelty

What is cruelty? Definitions are not always specific, but anyone with a modicum of common decency knows when a person has exceeded the bounds. The humane societies and enforcement organizations depend on notification from the public for instances of cruelty. If you know of or have good reason to suspect instances of animal mistreatment, talk to your local humane association officials. For answers and help with legal questions, see the Appendix.

Even a dog knows the difference between being tripped over, and being kicked.

— *Oliver Wendell Holmes*

Many dogs are killed when they jump or are thrown from the windows and backs of pickup trucks and cars. Pet stores and mail-order companies sell seat belts, harnesses, and car seats designed for pet travel protection.

• Opposite: American Staffordshire Terrier.

IT'S A DOG'S LIFE

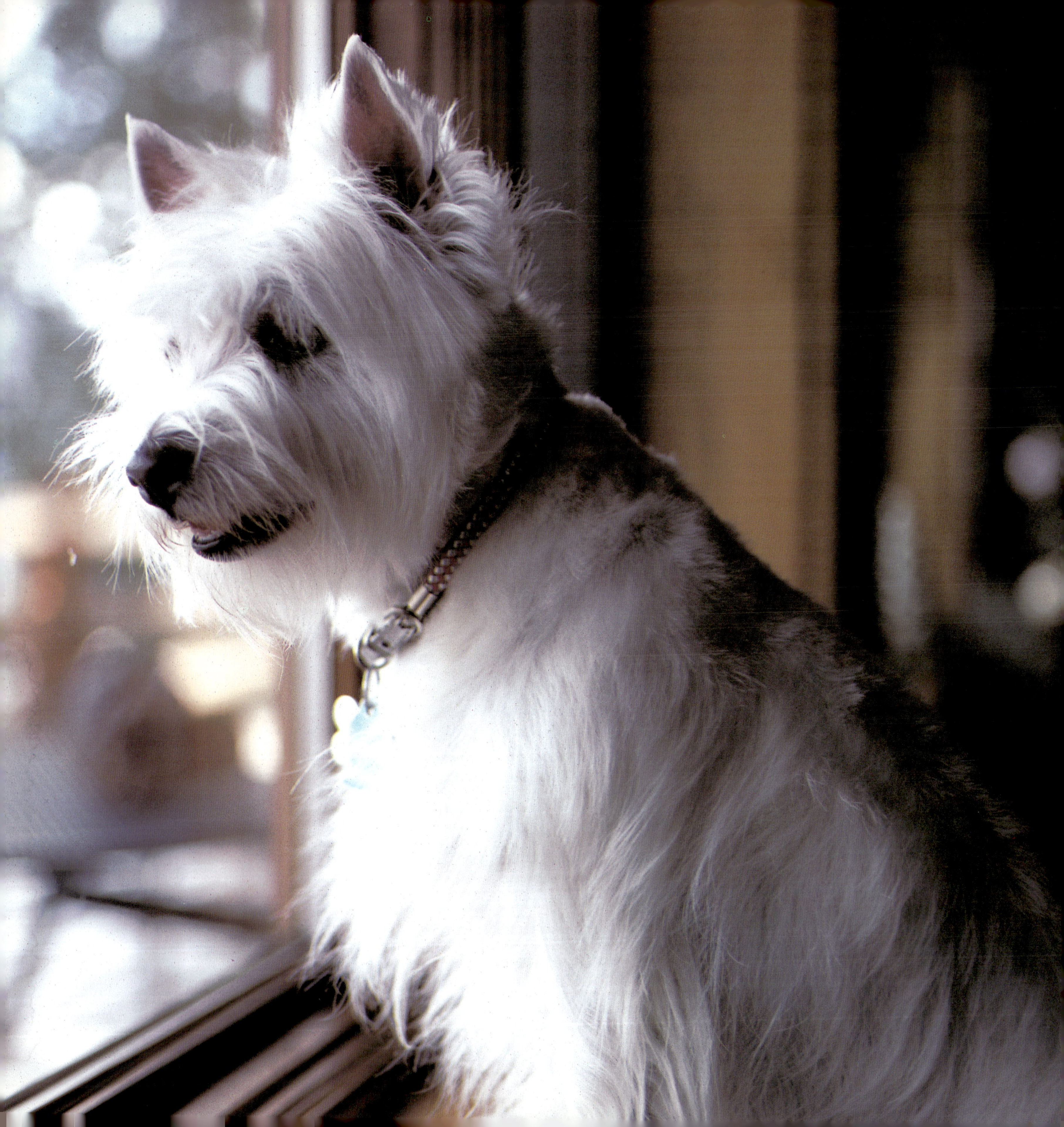

Let dogs delight to bark and bite, For God hath made them so.

—Isaac Watts (1674–1748)

CHAPTER FOUR

CANINE CARE

All veterinarians are qualified to treat your dog, but charges and specializations vary. Just as important is the doctor's personality, which should inspire confidence and trust in both you and your pet. The best recommendations come from other dog owners. Be as careful in selecting a veterinarian as you were choosing your pet; after all, your dog's health is at stake. Please note that veterinary medicine is constantly improving, and information quickly becomes obsolete. The following material is meant only as a guide; consult your veterinarian for the most current information.

Acupuncture, herbal therapy, chiropractic and even psychiatric treatments are available for your pet.

• Opposite: West Highland White Terrier.

• Above: Dogs are exposed to parasites while hunting or roaming.

THE HEALTHY DOG

Have your puppy examined as soon as you get it. Puppies are particularly susceptible to disease, and are vaccinated by a series of booster shots two weeks apart (just like human babies), with the first given at six to eight weeks. Once the series has been completed, yearly vaccinations protect adult dogs thereafter.

Routine Vaccinations

Your puppy should be vaccinated against the following common canine diseases. Distemper is a deadly viral disease affecting a dog's respiratory, intestinal, and central nervous systems; symptoms include yellowish diarrhea, thick discharge from the eyes and nose, and seizures. Infectious hepatitis affects the liver, and Leptospirosis attacks the digestive tract, liver, and kidneys. Infectious tracheobronchitis (kennel cough) is a respiratory disease that causes chronic coughing. Both parvo virus and corona virus can be deadly to puppies; symptoms include bloody diarrhea, vomiting, and severe dehydration. Rabies acts on the nervous system and results in paralysis and death. All these diseases are extremely contagious, yet easily preventable with proper vaccinations.

Altering Your Dog

Dogs are usually altered at six to nine months of age, but some early spay/neuter programs provide sterilization as early as six weeks. Surgery is performed under general anesthetic; some dogs are sore for a day or two afterward, and others exhibit no tenderness at all.

An ovariohysterectomy removes the female reproductive organs. A small incision is made on the dog's shaved and sterilized abdomen, then the Y-shaped uterus and ovaries are drawn out, tied off, and detached from inside the lower abdomen. Stitches are removed in seven to ten days.

Neutering removes the testicles from the male's scrotal sack. An incision is made in the shaved, sterilized skin of the penis just forward of the scrotum. The testicles are expressed, drawn out, and removed through this one small incision. Stitches are removed in seven to ten days.

Sterilization is often a requirement of shelter adoptions, and many agencies provide certificates for reduced-cost surgeries that most veterinarians gladly honor.

Common External Parasites

Most dogs get external parasites from contact with other infested dogs. Mange is caused by demodectic or sarcoptic mites that burrow beneath the dog's skin. Infestation commonly causes itchy sores and hair loss, sometimes serious skin infections, and occasionally death.

Ear mites live inside the ear canal, and feed by piercing the skin and sucking lymph. A black, tarry exudate forms inside the ear. Mites contribute to infection by causing irritation and inflammation.

Flies bite and torture, typically leaving ear tips scabbed and crusty. Flies also lay eggs in dirty or infected ears and skin, and the resulting maggots actually eat away the dog's flesh and can severely damage and even kill your dog.

The testicles descend into the scrotum at about ten days after birth, but are occasionally retained. Such cryptorchid dogs have a higher risk of testicular cancer and should always be neutered.

Lice cause intense itching, and are spread from contact with an infected animal. The flea is the top complaint of pet owners and primarily causes allergic reactions (scratching), and tapeworms. Ticks are bloodsucking parasites that attach to the skin like tiny balloons. Ticks cause painful lesions and spread diseases like canine ehrlichiosis, lyme disease, tick paralysis, and Rocky Mountain spotted fever. External parasites can be eliminated and controlled with proper administration of insecticides.

- Below: Ticks commonly attach inside a dog's ears and along the spine beneath the fur.

CANINE CARE

Poison!

Be extremely careful with insecticides, cleaning compounds, and any other chemicals; sweet-tasting antifreeze may lure a dog to drink, but destroys kidneys and quickly brings death. Signs of poisoning may include abdominal pain, diarrhea or vomiting, lack of coordination, drunken behavior, convulsions, or difficult breathing. If you suspect poisoning, call your veterinarian for instructions on specific action.

Common Internal Parasites

Dogs get tapeworms from swallowing infected fleas or from eating wild animals. Flea control prevents most tapeworm infestation and recurrence. Tapeworm segments look like dried grains of rice that stick to the anal area of your dog's fur.

Most internal parasites are contracted when a dog licks or sniffs contaminated ground; puppies often get worms from their mother before birth or as they nurse. Hookworms cause weight loss, severe anemia, and often death in puppies. Roundworms live in the stomach or intestines and look like strings of spaghetti when passed in the stool; in large numbers they cause intestinal damage and prevent food digestion. Whipworms produce diarrhea, anemia, weight loss, and weakness. Coccidiosis is a protozoan infection prompting bloody diarrhea and dehydration, and can cause severe debilitation in puppies. Giardia are contracted by drinking infected water, and also cause diarrhea. Intestinal parasites are eliminated and prevented with proper veterinary treatment.

Canine heartworms are blood parasites transmitted by mosquitoes from dog to dog. They enter the bloodstream as larva (microfilaria), then mature and plug the heart, ultimately causing death. Several preventatives are available; your veterinarian can help you decide which option is best for your pet.

- Below: Puppies are at the greatest risk for fatal health problems.

Grooming removes dead hair and loose dander, reduces shedding, and stimulates and distributes natural oils. Many breeds demand special hair care. Marion Hunt urges, "Inspect the premises for cleanliness and professionalism, and don't hesitate to ask questions. Tranquilizers potentially have risks, and should therefore only be used when a veterinarian is on the premises. Go by word of mouth to find a reputable, knowledgeable groomer."

A DOG'S LIFE

OTHER CANINE HEALTH CONCERNS

It's estimated that 25 percent of all dog disorders are related to seasonal allergies. Allergic skin is the equivalent of hay fever in people; instead of sneezing with runny nose and eyes, the allergic pet itches. Many dogs react violently to the chemical in "flea saliva," and it takes only one bite to set off an allergic reaction.

Bloat primarily affects large dogs, causing the stomach to swell or twist. Usually, affected dogs have eaten a big meal, drunk large amounts of water, and then exercised within a two to three hour period. Symptoms include restlessness, salivation and drooling, unsuccessful attempts to vomit, and a distended abdomen. Without immediate treatment, painful death quickly occurs.

Diabetes mellitus results when the pancreas doesn't produce enough insulin. Excessive fat can suppress insulin production, and overweight dogs may become diabetic as a direct result of being fat. Without insulin to move glucose into the cells of the body, diabetic dogs can't metabolize food; their appetite increases, but they lose weight. Eventually, the body is forced to find other food sources, and begins burning its own fat and muscle tissue (catabolism). Animals that have progressed to catabolism can rarely be saved. The diabetic dog often has cataracts, increased drinking, eating, and urination habits, and dramatic weight loss. Treatment is insulin injections with exercise and dietary management.

When the brain's electrical impulses "short circuit" normal neural processes, seizures may result. Epilepsy is a common clinical problem requiring medical management in small animals.

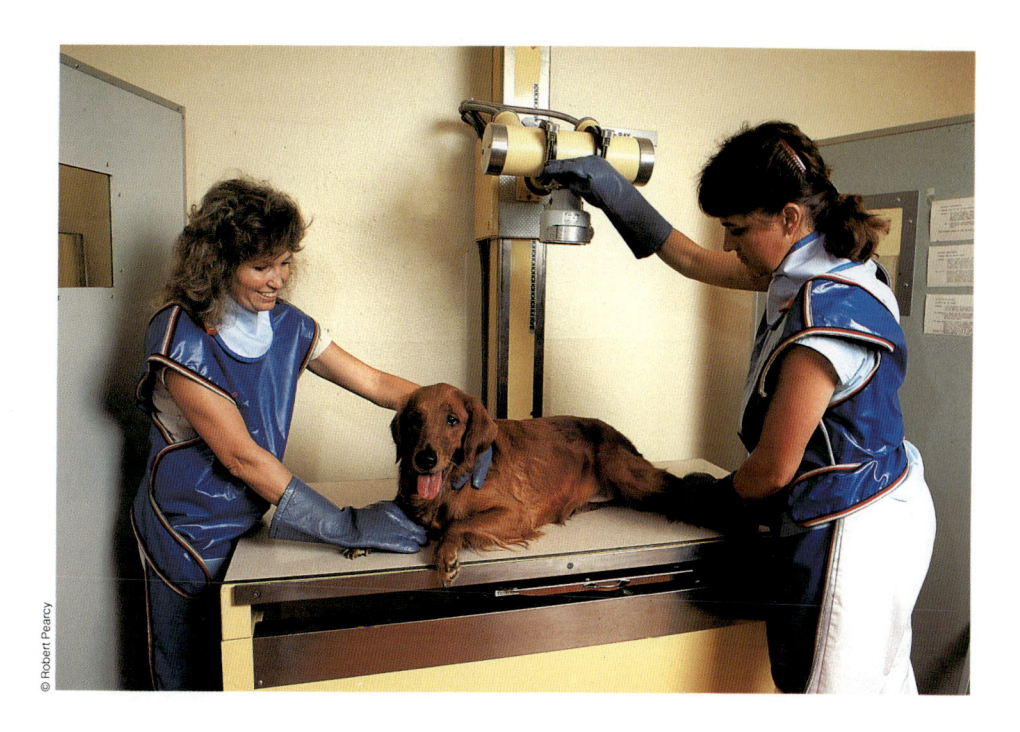

Ask your veterinarian about health insurance for your pet.

Heat stroke occurs when the dog becomes overheated. Dogs left in closed cars are prime candidates. Signs include shallow, rapid respiration, a rapid heart beat, and a temperature above 104°F (40°C). Cool the dog as quickly as possible (spray with water, pack with ice), and get it to a veterinarian immediately.

Hip dysplasia is a condition in which the hip socket and head of the femur fit improperly, causing lameness. Signs include hip pain, a limping or wavering gait, a hopping run, and difficulty rising. Hip dysplasia ranges from severe to minor, and is often an inherited tendency. Surgery can correct severe forms of the condition, and medication may give relief to minor discomfort.

Hot spots are a common problem occurring most often in the summer. Typically a round, red, hairless area develops on the skin. The area may emit clear

• Above: A Golden Retriever being x-rayed.

CANINE CARE

Seek recommendations from other pet owners for reputable boarding facilities. Kennels should be clean and safe, provide adequate room and care, and have a veterinarian on call.

fluid or pus. By chewing at it, dogs aggravate the area, and the infection quickly spreads. Hot spots must be treated immediately, or they will become severe.

Pancreatitis is the inflammation of the pancreas, and commonly occurs in underexercised, overweight dogs (usually over age two) that are habitually fed a diet of fatty foods, such as table scraps. Symptoms include diarrhea, nausea, and vomiting after eating.

Treating the Sick Dog

Pain, fever, and behavior changes are the earliest signs of ill health in dogs. The best way to recognize illness is to be familiar with your dog's healthy behavior. Consult a veterinarian any time you suspect a problem; better a false alarm than a dead dog.

A very fast heart rate indicates fever, anemia, shock, and any number of other problems. Normally the heart beats seventy to 130 times a minute in a resting dog (the smaller the dog, the faster the rate.) Take a dog's pulse by placing fingers or palm on its chest just behind and level with the left elbow.

Elimination habits are excellent indications of health and illness. Normal urine is clear yellow, and feces are usually brown and well formed. Foul smelling and/or loose stools, or stools containing mucous or blood (black, tarry stools) are abnormal. Persistent diarrhea or constipation, or changes in the amount or frequency of urination are all indications of potential illness that should be addressed by a veterinarian.

Normal adult-dog body temperature ranges from 101° to 102.5°F (38° to 39°C). To take your dog's temperature, lubricate a rectal thermometer with mineral oil or vaseline, place dog in standing position, lift the tail, and insert thermometer into the anus. Leave in place for about three minutes before reading.

Emergencies

Injured dogs may bite even a beloved owner out of fear or pain. Muzzle an injured dog for safety, using pantyhose, a long gauze bandage, or other soft cloth. Loop the material around the dog's muzzle and knot tightly over its nose. Bring the ends down under the chin and tie again; then pull the ends back around the dog's head and knot behind its ears.

Whenever a dog stops breathing, time is of the essence. Clear the dog's mouth, check for foreign bodies, and remove them if possible. Place a palm over the dog's chest immediately behind its left elbow, with your other palm on top; press firmly, then quickly release. Repeat every five seconds. If you can't hear breath moving in and out, mouth-to-nose respiration may also work. First clear the dog's mouth and throat; pull its tongue forward, then close the mouth. Place your lips over the dog's nose, and gently blow for three seconds. Repeat every two to three seconds.

Medicating Your Dog

Hiding pills in a dog's food doesn't always work. To pill a dog, grasp its muzzle firmly with your left hand. Curl your palm across the top of its muzzle so your thumb and index (or middle) finger encircle its muzzle and fit behind each upper canine tooth. Pressing on the dog's lips should cause its lower jaw to open; gently squeezing a finger against the roof of its mouth also works. Insert the pill way back on the center of the tongue, then close and hold the mouth shut

A DOG'S LIFE

while stroking its throat; dogs often lick their nose after swallowing. If the dog spits the pill out, try again until you're successful. To give liquid medicine, tilt the head to a 45° angle, then insert the applicator nozzle (dropper or syringe) into the dog's cheek pouch at the corner of the mouth. Keep the head elevated, and administer additional medication only after it has swallowed the initial amount.

The Geriatric Dog

The oldest dog on record was an Australian cattle dog that lived twenty-nine years, five months.

As veterinary health care improves, pets are living longer, healthier lives. The dog's average life span is twelve years, but smaller dogs often live longer. Although older pets must live with some afflictions of age, you can prevent some problems during your dog's senior years to prolong a cherished friend's life.

Arthritis occurs commonly in older dogs, stiffening joints and making movement painful. Pain is made worse by cold, a sudden change in the weather, or heavy exercise. There is no known cure, but medication may make your pet more comfortable.

Cancer is common in older pets. Breast cancer may affect older, intact female dogs. Skin tumors and oral tumors are just as dangerous. If you find a lump or bump, don't wait—see your veterinarian immediately.

Heart disease affects a third of all older dogs. Congestive heart failure is seen in 75 percent of all dogs over the age of nine. Early signs include exercise intolerance, shortness of breath, and coughing. In later stages, the dog may lose weight, have fainting spells, and swell with fluid. Without treatment, the dog will eventually die.

Hypothyroidism is caused when the thyroid gland fails to secrete enough thyroid hormone, resulting in an inhibited metabolic rate; symptoms include hair loss and recurrent skin infections, listlessness and depression, weight gain and obesity, and problems staying warm. Treatment consists of thyroid-hormone replacement tablets.

Periodontal disease strikes more than 85 percent of adult dogs. This silent destroyer may affect your dog's heart, liver, and kidneys with severe problems. An affected dog may have bad breath, and the pain will make it stop eating, salivate, and show much distress. Regular brushing of teeth (kits are available) and annual veterinary cleaning are recommended.

The older dog may seem moody and disoriented as its senses become less acute: eyesight dims; hearing weakens; things just don't smell as good as they used to. It may have trouble controlling bowel or bladder function. Veterinary medicine has made extraordinary advances, but treatment of an aging animal aims to ensure the quality of life, not merely prolong it. However, sometimes euthanasia is the better course of action.

• Center: Older dogs, like this elderly Malamute, need special care.

CANINE CARE

*...You were never masters, but friends.
I was your friend.
I loved you well, and was loved. Deep love endures to the end and far past the end. If this is my end, I am not lonely. I am not afraid. I am still yours.*

*—Robinson Jeffers,
from "The House Dog's Grave"*

Euthanasia

Puppies are born; they grow old; they die. Tragic accidents may take them too soon; they may drift away in the gentle sleep of old age; or they may linger in pain, begging silently for relief with suffering, questioning eyes.

When sickness or injury consumes your dog and there is little hope for recovery; when it knows its fight is done, and only a nameless yearning remains; when selfishly sustaining its life merely prolongs its pain; the determination to end its suffering is a decision only you, as a best friend, can make.

Euthanasia answers the sick dog's yearning with a single painless needle prick. Veterinarians often allow you to remain and comfort your dog as the medication is administered. You loved your dog best in life; that same love will tell you when it's time to end its pain. Have faith in your love; it's all your pet ever wanted, and it needs it now more than ever.

No other will ever take a cherished dog's place, but the sadness you feel upon your pet's death will grow sweeter with time. By and by, honor your dog's memory by opening your heart to another. So many yearn to be somebody's dog—love like yours should not be wasted.

THE DOG BOUTIQUE

Dog houses have gone beyond the simply practical; they now reach for the ultimate in fashion. There are decorated canvas tepees, fiberglass igloos (insulated with nitrogen), log cabins, and solar houses with built-in drainage, heat pumps, and air-conditioners; and even houses with flip-top roofs for those nice, sunny dog-day afternoons. And if your dog becomes bored with the view, you can install a window (dog level, of course) in the backyard fence. Some dogs even have their own hot tubs and personal masseurs to ease the aches and pains of arthritis.

A variety of beds is available as well; the old blanket in the corner isn't good enough any more. The modern pampered dog can choose from heated water beds, cedar-stuffed pillows (great flea deterrent), bunk beds

• Above: There are many stories of dogs who mourn the passing of their masters.

A DOG'S LIFE

(with attached ladder, naturally), day beds complete with coordinated dust ruffle, and even hammocks.

Likewise, dog bowls come in all colors, shapes, and sizes, and can be personalized with your pet's name and portrait. Special bowls are designed to keep fluffy ears from dragging in the food; heated bowls keep water from freezing during the winter; water and food dispensers make self-feeding easy. Trendy macrobiotic and holistic foods may be the vogue, but be sure to check them with a veterinarian to be sure they're safe. And don't forget the canine caterer to celebrate birthdays and obedience school graduation parties.

The utilitarian leather collar, harness, and leash are old hat; today, the "dogue-in-vogue" has a choice of leather or fabric, with rhinestones (or real stones) and even battery-powered collars that light up so the fashionable dog can be seen on evening walks. They come in every color, even Day-Glo, to make accessorizing that perfect look a little easier.

The pet psychic can help you discover your dog's particular taste. "Doggie Tees" offers T-shirts with your dog's favorite pro football team logo. And what sports fanatic would be caught dead without a matching hat? The Top-Dog Hat comes in six sizes and is cut to fit around canine ears and doggy chins. If it rains, they won't call the game, because Bark Avenue Fashions offers the Niagara Falls Rainsuit (with hood) for just such an occasion. The Houndware Store has life preservers for aquatically inclined canines; Custom Cover-Up has a line of matching yours-and-theirs dog wear, so everyone will know the two of you belong together.

There are backpacks for dogs to carry their own weight, and front packs for terrier-toting. If you crave the ultimate in togetherness, why not take your dog to camp? Honey Loring of Putney, Vermont, runs Camp Gone-to-the-Dogs each summer as a fun retreat for dogs and their owners. Camp offers obedience classes, games of fly-ball, swimming, frisbee, and general dog enjoyment. The agility course, where an owner must do everything his dog does, is a special favorite. There are also seminars on dog behavior and psychology, and even bereavement counseling.

Check magazine classified sections for other wonderful dog paraphernalia: the Earthquake Kit for pets; the bone-shaped "Santa Paws" Christmas stocking; a dog window shelf for perching and watching the world go by; the "Pet-Chime" indoor doorbell for when your pet needs to go out, and the "Kanine Korner" redwood fire hydrant with glow-in-the-dark base to show your pet where to go. My personal favorite is the "Yuppy Puppy" doggy-treat gumball machine that allows your dog to dispense treats. If your pet overindulges, you'll need to find some doggy "lean cuisine" as well.

• Below: Despite the snow, this Golden Retriever seems quite content in his happy home.

CANINE CARE

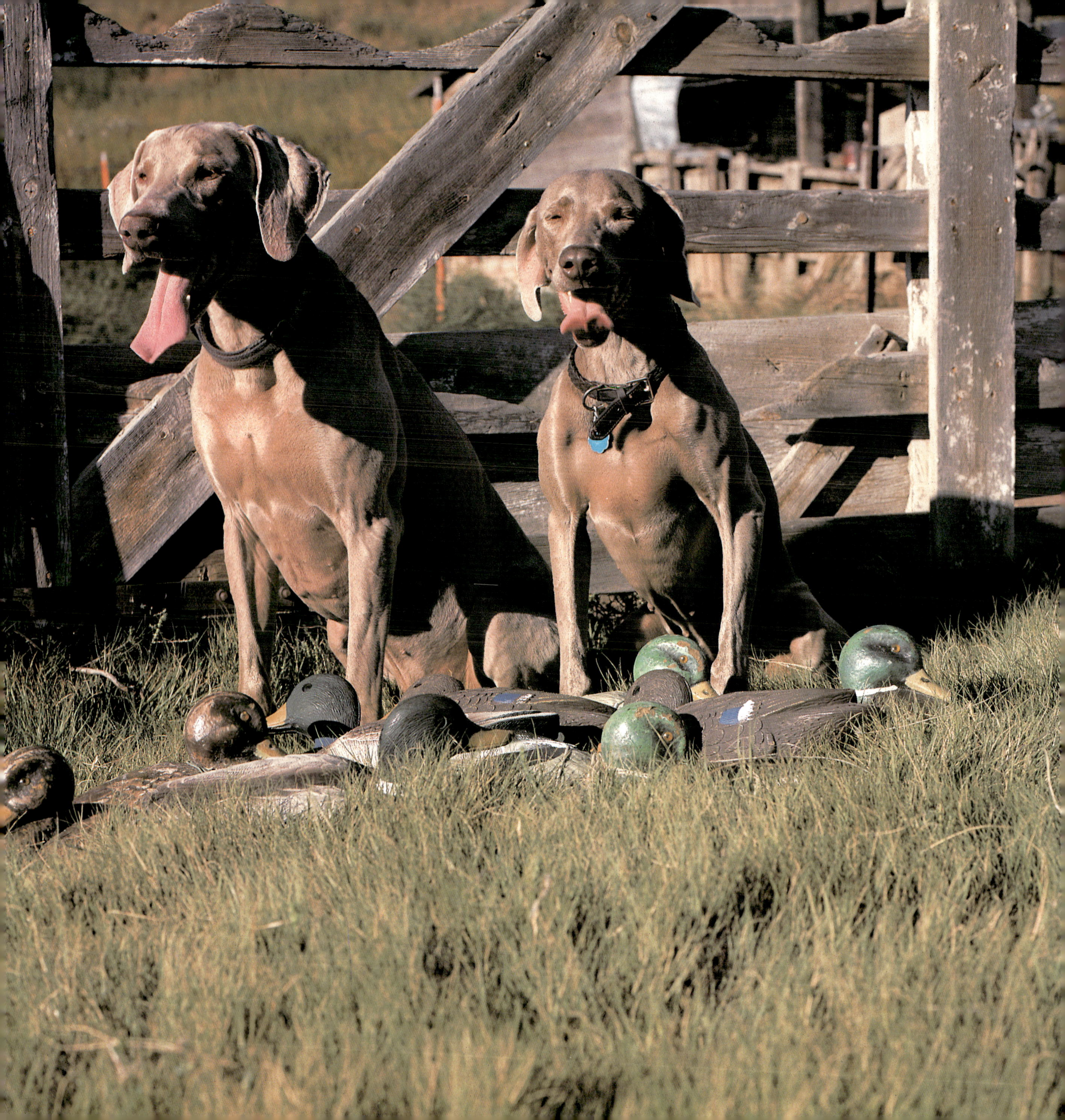

CHAPTER FIVE

A GALLERY OF DOGS

Now comes the hard part: which dog is right for you? A cute puppy, or a settled adult? The predictable temperament and striking features of a purebred, or a robust mutt? Dogs vary from pony- to pocket-sized, Whippet-thin to burly. They have foxy or accordion mugs, and tails that are long and thin, short and stout, curled, twisted, or nonexistent. Whatever your preference, a dog that's perfect for you is just waiting to be found.

Choose a breed that best fits your life-style. Honest breeders are willing to discuss potential problems as well as good points; they'll tell you about grooming and exercise requirements, temperament and trainability, and any breed-prone health problems. Marion Hunt of Pat-Mar Kennels, says, "If you aren't allowed to inspect the kennels, run! They may be hiding inadequate housing or care." A good breeder will be as concerned about your qualifications to provide a good home as you are to obtain a healthy, happy puppy.

• Opposite: Weimaraner dogs.

Above: Irish Wolfhound. Opposite page: Afghan Hound.

That's About the Size of It!

The tallest breeds are the Great Dane and Irish Wolfhound, but the heaviest are the Old English Mastiff and St. Bernard. Acromegaly (giantism) is a common mutation that produces massive bones and muscles; facial skin grows out of proportion, producing the wrinkly, jowly appearance of the Bloodhound.

The smallest breeds are miniature versions of the Yorkshire Terrier, Chihuahua, and Toy Poodle; the Japanese Imperial Ch'in standards call for the smaller the better. Midget animals' heads are proportionally large to accommodate a normal-size brain, but otherwise they're just small versions of larger breeds. Achondroplasia (dwarfism) causes bones to grow into curved, stunted limbs, as in the Basset and Dachshund; early cessation of facial bone growth produces the pug nose, large head, and stubby paws found in Bulldogs.

Expect the breeder to ask pointed questions, and answer them honestly.

There are about 400 distinct breeds of purebred dogs in the world. The American Kennel Club (AKC) recognizes 130 and lists ten miscellaneous breeds; the United Kennel Club (UKC) recognizes 147; and the Canadian Kennel Club (CKC) registers 148 and lists about 143 miscellaneous breeds. Miscellaneous breeds aren't eligible for registration until sustained interest in, and healthy, dynamic growth of the breed has been determined by the registering association. Note: Specific standards may vary from one association to another, and breeds registered by one may not be recognized in others. AKC emphasizes conformity, while the UKC stresses performance and working-dog breeds. The AKC, UKC, and CKC are affiliations of hundreds of local all-breed clubs, national specialty-breed clubs, obedience clubs, and sanctioned national dog sport associations; these smaller clubs put on dog shows.

Any dog, whether mutt or purebred, is eligible for obedience trials and championships.

There's simply not enough space to do justice to all 400 breeds. The following gallery section offers only general, brief information for many popular favorites. Contact the AKC, UKC, and/or CKC for detailed descriptions, standards, and histories of recognized breeds, and for location of clubs and breeders.

A DOG'S LIFE

American Kennel Club (AKC)
51 Madison Avenue
New York, NY 10010

Australian National Kennel Council (ANKC)
Royal Show Grounds
Ascot Vale, Victoria
Australia

Canadian Kennel Club (CKC)
2150 Bloor Street, West
Toronto, Ontario M6S 4Z7

International Federation of Kennel Clubs
(Fédération Cynologique Internationale)
14, rue Leopold II
13-6530 Thuin, Belgium

Kennel Club (KC)
1 Clarges Street
London W1Y 8AB
England

New Zealand Kennel Club (NZKC)
Private Bag
Porirva, New Zealand

United Kennel Club (UKC)
100 East Kilgore Road
Kalamazoo, MI 49001-5598

GALLERY

Size key: Height at the shoulder

Small = 15 inches (37.5cm) or less

Medium = 16 to 22 inches (40 to 55cm)

Large = above 23 inches (57.5cm)

Generally, hounds are rather independent, indifferent to human control, and like to roam; their barks and bays make them a bit noisy around the house. Most spaniels, retrievers, and pointers are too friendly to make good watchdogs; Weimaraners, Chesapeake Bay Retrievers, and American Water Spaniels are the exceptions. Guard dogs have high energy levels, meaning that they require lots of exercise; they're quick to learn, but often stubborn. Draft dog breeds are generally quiet and docile, and easy to train and live with. Most terriers are small, very active, aggressive dogs that need much attention; they like to bark, making them excellent watchdogs. Herding dogs have high energy levels, are easy to train and live with, and are devoted. Sled dogs may bark at intruders, but are so friendly they'd probably show a burglar where the silver is hidden, and even help load it in his car.

Affenpinscher

This small compact dog is covered with black (usually) wiry fur. Affenpinscher means "monkey dog," and this dog's flat, whiskery face, bushy eyebrows, and round dark eyes are indeed a bit simian. It is generally a quiet, devoted little dog.

Afghan Hound

The Afghan is a large, dignified-looking sight hound (bred to chase prey by sight) with a stunning coat of long, beautiful, silky fur that requires regular grooming. The aristocratic Afghan tends to think for itself, but makes a wonderful companion.

Airedale Terrier

The "King of Terriers" is the largest terrier, with a long, flat head, powerful jaws, and hard, dense wiry fur in shades of brown, black, and tan. Originally bred in the nineteenth century to control the otter population on the Aire River in Yorkshire, the Airedale loves water. This dog is sweet tempered, with a dignified aloofness.

Akita

This large dog has a handsome bearlike head, curled tail, and thick medium-length fur. Its origins lie in old Japan, where Akitas were used to hunt large animals such as bear and deer. The Akita is a very loving, faithful, and fastidious dog that needs firm training and regular exercise; it is sometimes aggressive toward other dogs.

• Above: Airedale. Right: Alaskan Malamute.

Alaskan Malamute

Malamutes are the largest of sled dogs. The wolflike head has a distinctive white cap or mask, and its thick fur makes it a heavy year-round shedder. Powerfully built and intelligent, Malamutes are also extremely clean and very fond of children.

American Eskimo, Standard and Miniature

The American Eskimo, nicknamed "The Dog Beautiful," may be either small- or medium-sized and looks like a miniature Samoyed. This curious, gregarious, occasionally headstrong dog wants to be in on everything.

A DOG'S LIFE

American Staffordshire Terrier ("Pit Bull")

This handsome, impressive, medium-sized dog tragically is best known for illegal use in dog fights. These dogs are not naturally hostile; although often aggressive with other dogs, they're usually gentle, loyal, and extremely affectionate when correctly socialized.

Australian Shepherd

Aussies are gorgeous medium-sized, long-furred dogs resembling small Collies, but with almost no tail. They are an extremely intelligent working breed.

Basenji

The Basenji is an ancient dog, native to North Africa. It is a medium-sized dog with pricked ears, a wrinkled, intelligent face, curled tail, and short, very fine, sleek fur. The Basenji cleans itself like a cat; it doesn't bark, but chortles and yodels. Basenjis make endearing, courageous, playful yet gentle pets.

Basset Hound

This is a hefty, medium-sized, deep-voiced dog with a smooth, short coat that moves ponderously on very short legs, making it an excellent tracker. Bassets have extremely long ears that "sweep the morning dew"; they are gentle, affectionate, good-mannered dogs.

Beagle

This cheerful little hound, known for its hunting abilities since Elizabethan times, may be either small or medium-sized, and has never met a stranger. Despite its size, it likes lots of running room, and lives for sniffing.

Bearded Collie

The medium-sized Beardie wears a quizzical expression on its bearded face and is full of high energy and spirits. This long-coated dog makes a stable, self-confident, devoted family pet.

Bedlington Terrier

A lamb look-alike, the Bedlington is a hardy, medium dog. Developed by miners in nineteenth-century England, it was used to eliminate vermin from the mines. Its pear-shaped head and mild, gentle expression are endearing; it walks with a mincing springy step, and has thick, soft stand-up fur.

• Far left: Basenji. Top, right: Beagle. Bottom, right: Basset Hound.

A GALLERY OF DOGS

105

Belgian Sheepdogs

The Groenendael is a large, solid black dog that looks like a long-haired German Shepherd. The Tervuren looks the same, with fawn to mahogany fur with black tips. The rare Laekenois has a rough, tan coat; the Malinois looks like a short-coated German Shepherd. These gorgeous breeds are year-round shedders. They are extremely trainable, always in motion, affectionate and friendly, and extremely possessive.

Bernese Mountain Dog

This is a large Mastiff–type black dog with white and tan markings on a wavy, long silky coat. The Bernese is an exceptionally faithful, hardy dog that needs human companionship.

Bichon Frise

The sturdy Bichon is a small, bouncy, snow-white powder-puff of a dog with black merry eyes; its full beard makes it look like Santa Claus. The Bichon Frise does not shed, but its silky hair requires regular grooming. Once a pampered favorite of European courtiers, the Bichon is smart and devoted—an excellent pet— and good for allergy-sufferers, too.

Bloodhound

Bloodhounds are powerful, large, formidable tracking dogs, with characteristic loose facial skin that hangs in deep folds. Puppies have been known to trip over their own ears. This is a reserved but good-tempered dog that's gentle with children.

Border Collie

Originally a Scottish herding dog, this medium- to large-sized, extremely intelligent, loyal worker resembles a small Collie with a broad muzzle. Mike the Border Collie starred in the movie *Down and Out In Beverly Hills*.

Borzoi (Russian Wolfhound)

The elegant Borzoi is a large sight hound similar in type to the Greyhound, but with long fur. It was developed in Russia in the thirteenth century. This quiet, gentle aristocrat is easy to train and makes an excellent companion.

• Above: Groenendael puppy. Bottom, right: Bernese Mountain Dog.

A DOG'S LIFE

Boston Terrier

The small "Boston Gentleman" is a saucy scamp with boundless energy that stands up to anything. It resembles a tiny Boxer, except for the screw tail and distinctive two-tone coat that looks like a tuxedo. Bostons make wonderful house pets; however, they share the breathing problems of all flat-nosed breeds.

Bouvier des Flandres

This large dog's roughly tousled, harsh, wiry fur makes it look like an unshorn giant Schnauzer. Bred as a cattle herder in Flanders, it is spirited and bold, but well behaved and fearless.

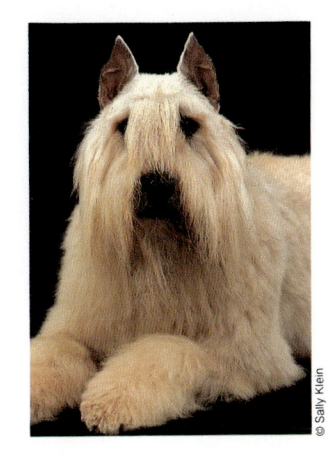

Boxer

Boxers are sturdy, medium-sized, squarely built dogs, with deep facial wrinkles, cropped ears, docked tail, undershot jaw, and short, tight fur. Nineteenth-century German breeders developed the Boxer as a police dog of intelligence and courage. Boxers have a playful temperament; they're wary of strangers, but make friends easily.

Briard

This large, hairy dog is often described as a heart wrapped in fur—6 inches (15cm) of straight fur all over that needs lots of grooming. A very ancient French herding and guard dog, today's Briard is an independent, yet devoted pet.

Brittany Spaniel

The medium-sized Britt wants to hunt; it is a loving dog with little or no tail, covered with either dark orange and white, or liver and white wavy fur. It is very friendly, wants to please, and is an excellent dog for children.

Brussels Griffon

This small, rare dog has personality plus, and is a little larger than, but otherwise resembles, the Affenpinscher. Popular with nineteenth-century Belgian royalty, the Brussels Griffon is intelligent and independent.

• Top, left: Bouvier de Flandres. Bottom, left: Boxer puppy. Bottom, right: Brussels Griffon.

A GALLERY OF DOGS

Bulldog

The Bulldog is small to medium in stature, but very broad, powerful, and compact. Its massive head is proportionally larger than the rest of the body, and the flattened, wrinkled face makes it look like the dog ran into a wall. Despite a ferocious expression, Bulldogs have kind, dignified natures.

Cairn Terrier

The cheeky Cairn is a small, shaggy, compact dog, with a "weatherproof coat." This charmer is tempted to forge ahead on leash, and prone to barking. Toto from the *Wizard of Oz* was a Cairn Terrier.

- Left: Bulldog. Middle: Chinese Crested Dog. Right: Chow Chow. Opposite: Cairn Terrier puppy.

Cavalier King Charles Spaniel

This is the small beguiling dog favored by King Charles II of England and featured in many famous paintings. Large expressive eyes give it an endearing quality. These dogs are willing and even anxious to learn, with low excitability; shyness can be a problem.

Chihuahua

An ancient Mexican breed, the Chihuahua is an extremely small dog—it often weighs in at less than 2 pounds (0.9 kg). It has either short, smooth fur or a long, silky coat. Despite its dainty appearance, it has an alert, fierce, forceful personality and will challenge authority.

Chinese Crested Dog

This is a very clean, nearly bald, small dog that resembles the Chihuahua; it has minimal fur on the feet, head crest, and tail. It is excellent for allergy sufferers.

A DOG'S LIFE

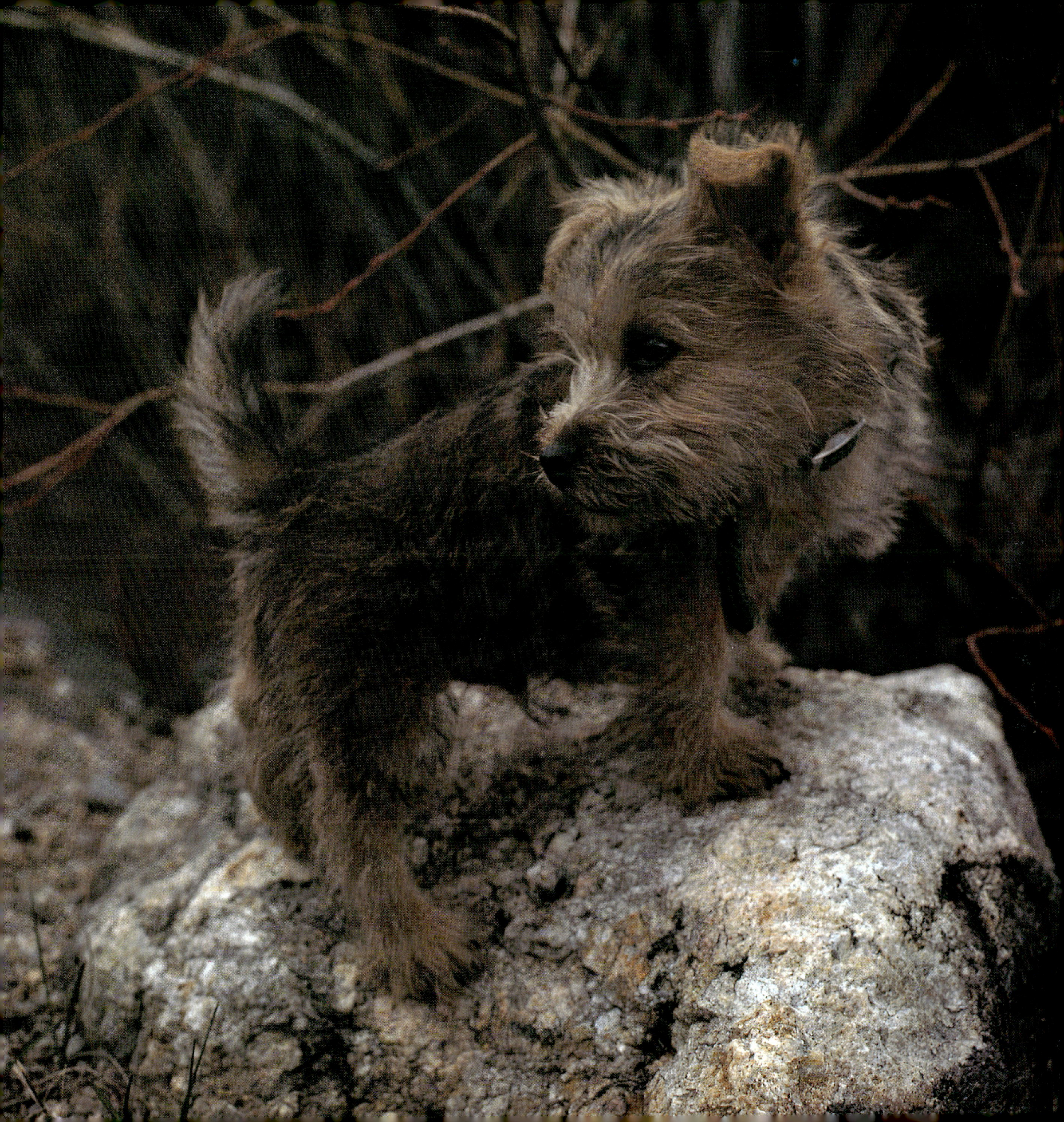

Chinese Shar-Pei

The sweet, lovable Shar-Pei is of medium or small stature, and is known for extraordinarily wrinkled, loose skin, a hippo-like face, a blue-black tongue, and a short, bristly coat. (Shar-Pei means "sandy coat.") Originally bred in China as fighting dogs, some Shar-Peis tend to be aggressive. Breeders are fighting a tendency toward eye problems.

Chow Chow

Chows are large, densely furred Chinese dogs that look like a cross between a lion and a bear. They are known for a blue-black tongue, scowling expression, and tightly curled tail. Chows are dignified, loyal pets with a reputation as one-person dogs. They're often reserved with strangers and sometimes aggressive with other dogs.

Clumber Spaniel

This thoughtful-looking, dignified large dog looks like a cross between a Cocker and Basset. It is an active, tireless retriever that moves with a rolling gait.

Cocker Spaniel

The very popular Cocker is a sturdy, small dog with a rounded head, long, elegant ears, and profuse, gorgeous fur. Cockers are prone to skin problems, cataracts, and hip dysplasia. Cockers are merry, laid-back, companionable dogs with a short docked tail constantly in happy motion.

Collie, Rough and Smooth

The "Lassie" stories popularized this large, strong, active shepherd; it has a distinctive, full, lush coat with a white-maned "collar." The Smooth Collie has a short coat, and looks more angular.

Dachshund

The small, muscular Dachshund has a long, svelte body set on short legs, and is either standard or miniature in size. Its coat may be smooth, long, or wire-haired. Originally used to flush badgers out of their holes, the Dachshund is active, very trainable, and occasionally pushy or stubborn. The Dachshund is both clever and courageous, and often gets into trouble just for fun. Early training is a must to keep an upper hand.

• Right: Collie puppy. Opposite, top: Dalmatian. Opposite, bottom left: Cocker Spaniel. Opposite, bottom right: Chinese Shar-Pei puppy.

A DOG'S LIFE

A GALLERY OF DOGS

111

- Below: Dandie Dinmont Terriers. Right: Wire-haired Fox Terrier.

Dalmatian

Dalmatians are large dogs with characteristic dark "polka dots" against white, short, smooth hair. They have a long and varied working history and are known for their affinity with horses. Dalmatians are prone to congenital deafness, and bladder and kidney stones. They are born white; the spots develop later. Dalmatians are very clean and loyal one-person/family dogs.

Dandie Dinmont Terrier

This hardy, fearless, small dog looks like a Dachshund with lots of crisp, soft hair. Dandies need regular grooming; they fit in anywhere.

Doberman Pinscher

The Doberman is a large dog with the agility, strength, and speed of a giant terrier. Its head is long and clean, its eyes deep and almond shaped, and its ears and tail cropped, and it has smooth, close-lying hair. Dobermans are extremely intelligent, loyal, fiercely protective, and devoted family dogs.

Dogue de Bordeaux

This large Mastiff-type breed is the national dog of France. The Dogue has a smooth, short, light-colored coat with black points.

Finnish Spitz

The medium-sized Finn looks like a fox. Finland's national dog, the Finn is lively and courageous; an excellent hunter. Barking can be a problem; sensitive and independent, the Finn is easily bored with repetition.

Flat-Coated Retriever

This large dog, a descendant of the Newfoundland, resembles a Labrador Retriever but with moderate-length, flat-lying fur; minimal grooming is required. Dependable and active, this is a heavy tail-wagger.

Foxhound

The Foxhound is a large dog with a fairly long, domed head, long pendulous ears, gay tail, and a close, hard, medium-length coat.

A DOG'S LIFE

Fox Terrier, Smooth and Wire-Haired

Fox Terriers are small to medium-sized white dogs with colored markings. The tail is docked long and held erect, and ears drop forward close to the cheek. The Wire-Haired Fox Terrier looks like a small Airedale. This is a gay, lively dog that gets excited at the least provocation.

German Shepherd Dog (Alsatian)

This is a large, noble dog that resembles a wolf; it's a heavy shedder year-round, and needs lots of exercise. Shepherds are prone to hip dysplasia, often have sensitive digestion, and occasionally suffer from epilepsy. Shepherds thrive on training; they are intelligent, eager to please, loyal, loving, protective, and fearless, yet cautious with strangers.

Golden Retriever

The Golden Retriever is a large dog with a broad head, moderately long fur, and a kind expression. Goldens crave attention and adore being with people; they'll submit to nearly anything just to be near their owners, and they adore children.

Great Dane

Danes are very large, reaching more than 30 inches (75cm) at the shoulder. This is a muscular dog with a refined Mastiff head, cropped ears, and short, thick, glossy fur. Danes tend to age rather quickly, and a wagging tail can be a bruising experience. Spirited and courageous, friendly and dependable, Danes make excellent pets, but you may go broke feeding them.

Great Pyrenees

The majestic white Pyrenees is a large Mastiff-type dog that often reaches 120 pounds (59kg), and moves with an ambling, rolling gait. It is very muscular and courageously protective, yet gentle and devoted to its family.

Greyhound

The elegant Greyhound is a large, very ancient Egyptian breed. Originally bred as a hunting dog, today the Greyhound is known for speed—up to 35 miles (56km) per hour. It is a quiet and clean pet, and is affectionate without fawning.

Ibizan Hound

This large dog looks like a Greyhound with upright ears. There is a wire-haired and a short-haired variety. They have pink noses and amber eyes. Friendly and active, Ibizans are excellent family dogs and are very healthy.

Irish and Gordon Setters

Legend holds that the Irish Setter arose "fully formed from among the shamrocks." This large dog has a distinctive, silky, rich chestnut to red coat. It has a puppyish exuberance and zest for life and needs a lot of exercise. The Gordon Setter looks similar, but is coal black with chestnut markings.

The tallest dog ever recorded was a Great Dane named Shamgret Danzas, who stood 41.5 inches (103cm) at the shoulder, and weighed 238 pounds (107kg).

- Center: Golden Retriever.

A GALLERY OF DOGS

Irish Water Spaniel

This large dog, with its coat of crisp tight ringlets, resembles a Standard Poodle with a long, fringeless tail. The Irisher is a one person/family dog, easily taught, eager, and enthusiastic.

Irish Wolfhound

This large dog often reaches 120 pounds (54kg) and resembles a very heavy Greyhound with wiry, rough textured fur in various solid colors. It is a gentle, brave, and dignified dog.

Italian Greyhound

The Italian is a small Greyhound, which can reach speeds of up to 40 miles (64km) per hour. It is intelligent, affectionate, and sensitive, and was a favorite of royalty throughout Europe during the nineteenth century.

Jack Russell Terrier

The Jack Russell is a small, tough, sporty dog full of confidence, and has mostly white with tan or black markings. Its ears are dark brown and almond shaped, and the docked tail is carried high.

Japanese Chin (Japanese Spaniel)

The Chin is a small, Pug-like dog with long, profuse black and white, or red and white fur. It carries a plumed tail draped over its back, and lifts its feet high as it walks. Long a favorite of Japan's emperors, it is a bright, alert, very clean dog that never forgets a friend— or an enemy!

Keeshond

The Keeshond has a dense, ash-gray, easily-cared-for coat. A Dutch breed, this is a most affectionate, lovable dog.

• Right: Jack Russell Terrier puppies.

A DOG'S LIFE
114

Kerry Blue Terrier

The medium-size Kerry Blue is the national dog of Ireland, and looks a little like the Airedale in shape. It has a distinctive soft, wavy blue-gray coat. Kerries are smart and lovable and make excellent watchdogs; they tend to fight other dogs.

Komondor

This is a large, 120-pound (54kg) dog with an unusual heavy, white, tassel-like corded coat. It looks like a mop on legs. Komondors are self-reliant, protective, earnest, and faithful dogs.

Kuvasz

The Hungarian Kuvasz is a large white dog very similar to the Great Pyrenees. Kuvasz means "protector"; these dogs demonstrate extremely strong protective responses toward children and are slow to make new friends.

Labrador Retriever

Labs are large, black, yellow, or chocolate-colored dogs with dense short coats and a distinctive broad "otter tail" that may bruise you when exuberantly wagged. Labs are strong, active dogs that need minimal grooming, are exceedingly friendly and excellent with children.

Lhasa Apso

This small, solid Pekingese-like dog has a screw tail carried well over the back, and lots of straight, hard hair, even over the face. Lhasas are watchful, hardy, easily trained, and obedient to those they trust.

Maltese

The fastidious Maltese is a small, solid-white dog with long pendant ears, a tail that arches over its back, and lots of silky straight fur that demands much grooming.

Manchester Terrier

This is a small dog that comes in standard and toy varieties, and resembles a long-tailed tiny Doberman. The Manchester is a wise, intelligent, sleek, and clean little dog.

- Above, left: Komondor.
Left: Yellow Labrador.

A GALLERY OF DOGS

The heaviest recorded dog ever was an Old English Mastiff named Zorba from London that weighed 319 pounds (174 kg). Nose to tail, Zorba measured an impressive 8 feet 3 inches (2.5m).

Mastiff

This is a very large, powerful dog reaching more than 30 inches (75cm) in height, with a square head, short, broad muzzle, and small ears that lie flat and close to the cheek. Mastiffs have short, close-lying fur in various colors, and are good-natured and courageous, yet docile.

Miniature Pinscher

The small "King of Toys" looks like a tiny Doberman Pinscher, and is a very alert, self-possessed watchdog. It is a bold, loving little dog that has a tendency to show off.

Newfoundland

The Newfoundland is a 130-pound (59kg) Mastiff-like dog with a moderately long black or bronze coat. It is a heavy shedder. Despite its size, the Newfoundland has a very gentle, docile nature.

Norwegian Elkhound

The Norwegian Elkhound is a large, spitz-type dog resembling the Keeshond, but with shorter fur, and is a friendly, energetic dog.

Old English Sheepdog

This large tailless dog has profuse, shaggy gray and white fur that covers the entire body, even the face and eyes; it needs careful and frequent grooming. The Old English Sheepdog has a distinctive ambling gait and a bell-like bark. It is a naturally exuberant and playful dog that demands attention and a daily romp.

Papillon

Think of a Japanese Chin with a foxy muzzle, and you get the small Papillon. Ears are frilled and carried like the spread wings of a "papillon," or butterfly. This is a friendly, hardy dog.

Pekingese

The small Pekingese was created when a lion "yielded to the caresses of a butterfly." This thick-set, short-legged dog has a wide, flat head and an extremely short, wrinkled nose; long, profuse straight hair cascades over the body, and the tail is carried over the back. Pekes are calm and good tempered; they condescend to strangers, but welcome a romp with the family.

• Above, right: Papillon.

A DOG'S LIFE

Pharaoh Hound

The Pharaoh is a large Greyhound-like dog with erect ears that can blush—the inside of the ears and nose go pink with excitement or happiness. Pharaohs are very affectionate.

Pomeranian

The Pomeranian is the smallest of the spitz breeds, and is a heavy shedder year-round. It is docile yet vivacious.

Poodle (Toy, Miniature, Standard)

This active, elegant dog is available in three sizes (small, medium, and large) and a variety of colors. Poodles don't shed, but grooming is necessary to achieve their distinctive appearance. Poodles are very smart and will train you in the blink of an eye, so stay on your toes.

Pug

The small Pug looks like a toy Mastiff with a curled tail. Some say the name derives from the Latin *pugnus*, meaning "fist," because its profile resembles a fist. The Pug lives for people, and has little or no odor.

Puli

This medium dog resembles the mop-coated Komondor, but with rusty black fur and a tail carried over the back. It's an affectionate, home-loving companion that is suspicious of strangers.

- Top: Pomeranian.
  Bottom: Poodle.

A GALLERY OF DOGS

Rhodesian Ridgeback

This is a large dog with a distinctive ridge of hair growing on its back. A clean, easily kept pet, the Rhodesian Ridgeback is never noisy and loves children.

Rottweiler

This compact, powerful dog is a large, mostly black, Mastiff-type dog with a broad, wrinkled head, docked tail, and ears that tip forward. It is bold and courageous, self-assured, slow to make friends, and protective of home and family.

Saint Bernard

This dog is another very large Mastiff type with long orange and white fur; a heavy year-round shedder. There's also a smooth-haired, short-coated variety.

Saluki

The Saluki is another large Greyhound type, but with long silky fur on the ears and tail. It is an ancient northern African and Asian breed, originally used for hunting. The Saluki is very catlike in the way it cleans itself. It is an aloof, one-family dog that learns quickly, but becomes easily bored.

- Left: Rhodesian Ridgeback puppies. Right: Rottweiler.

A DOG'S LIFE

Samoyed

A striking, gorgeous large white or cream-colored spitz-type dog originally bred in Siberia, the Samoyed is a heavy shedder year round. Samoyeds are excellent watchdogs, yet gentle and companionable.

Schipperke

Schipperkes are small to medium-sized cobby dogs (sturdy dogs with low-lying bodies on short, square legs) with a sharp expression and an air of self-importance. Once used as a watchdog on boats, they have a foxy head, a tailless, rounded rump, and a dense, harsh, black coat that forms a mane. The "little captain" (its name comes from the Flemish word for "skipper") is very fond of children, and will defend house and master against all comers.

Schnauzer (Giant, Standard, Miniature)

In all sizes, the Schnauzer is a nearly square dog, with cropped ears and erect, docked tail, bushy eyebrows, and whiskers. They are spirited, alert, clean, easily trained, and loyal.

Scottish Terrier

The small, thickset, wiry-coated Scottie has short legs, erect pointed ears, and a head that seems too long for its size.

Shetland Sheepdog

Shelties are small to medium-sized, extremely intelligent dogs. They look like miniature Collies. Shelties are intensely loyal, affectionate, and responsive, yet reserved with strangers.

Shih Tzu

This small, ancient Chinese dog looks similar to the Pekingese, but has much more facial hair. The Shih Tzu is often called the "chrysanthemum-faced dog" because its facial hair grows in all directions. This is a very active, alert dog with an arrogant carriage.

• Top: Scottish Terriers.
Bottom: Sheltie.

A GALLERY OF DOGS
119

Weimaraner

The large "gray ghost" is known for its shimmery gray coat, light-colored eyes and effortless movement. Loyal and obedient, it enjoys being in the middle of a family.

Welsh Corgi (Cardigan and Pembroke)

These small dogs, named for the Welsh towns where they were first bred, look like German Shepherds with sawed-off legs; the Pembroke has pointed ears and no tail, while the Cardigan has rounded ears, a full tail, and is a little larger. The Pembroke is known as the dog of the British Royal family. These dogs have big opinions of themselves, but are very agreeable house pets that need frequent exercise. Corgis require minimal grooming.

Siberian Husky

This is a large breed very similar in appearance to the Alaskan Malamute; developed as a sled dog, it is a heavy shedder year-round. Huskies are naturally friendly, gentle, very alert, quite clean, and sometimes independent.

West Highland White Terrier

The small snow-white Westie is shaped somewhere between the Cairn and the Scottish Terrier. A tough, brave, spunky dog originally bred for hunting small animals, the Westie is lively and demanding of attention. An ideal apartment dog, the Westie tends to be a barker and likes to dig, so beware.

Skye Terrier

The small Skye looks like a Dachshund, but with straight long fur hanging to the ground and over the face. It is generally a one-person dog. The Skye is distrustful of strangers, but it is not vicious.

Whippet

The Whippet is another medium-sized Greyhound look-alike, bred in nineteenth century England as a racer. Whippets are elegant, easy-to-train dogs that are small enough to carry. They have an easy-care, short coat.

Vizsla

This large dog is sometimes called the Hungarian Pointer, and looks like a smaller rusty-gold version of the Weimaraner. The Vizsla is an obedient and affectionate companion.

- Above: Siberian Husky.

A DOG'S LIFE

AFTERWORD

The Dog Companion has been a joy to write. I hope the tales and tips, frolics, and facts catalogued in its pages have not only answered many of your questions, but also whetted your appetite to learn more.

Learning about *Canis familiaris* is an exciting adventure. Becoming educated about the wonderful world of dogs makes us better pack leaders to each impish, playful, devoted furry wonder we would lead.

The dog has trotted the globe and traveled hundreds of centuries with humans, remaining ever faithful. Responsible dog-lovers like you will ensure that the dog keeps its envied position: the canine companion, pampered pet, valued partner, and above all, best friend.

The smallest mature dog ever recorded was a Yorkie from Great Britain that stood 2.5 inches (6.25cm) at the shoulder, measured 3.75 inches (9.3cm) from nose to tail, and weighed 4 ounces (112g).

Xoloitzcuintli

The Xolo (*show-low*), also known as the Mexican Hairless, resembles an oiled Chihuahua, but ranges from tiny to more than 60 pounds (27kg). Not all Xolos are completely bald. Many Xolos prefer an odd resting posture of butt up, front end down. Xolos have a sweet, sensitive personality and need to be with people. They love to play tricks. Tiny Xolos enjoy perching on shoulders.

Yorkshire Terrier

The Yorkie is a small, very compact dog with erect ears, docked tail, and long, perfectly straight metallic fur. Cuteness allows the highly intelligent Yorkie to manipulate owners into all kinds of concessions. Show dogs need lots of grooming. Yorkies have a devastatingly shrill bark that neighbors don't appreciate.

• Left: Whippet. Right: Yorkshire Terrier puppies.

A GALLERY OF DOGS

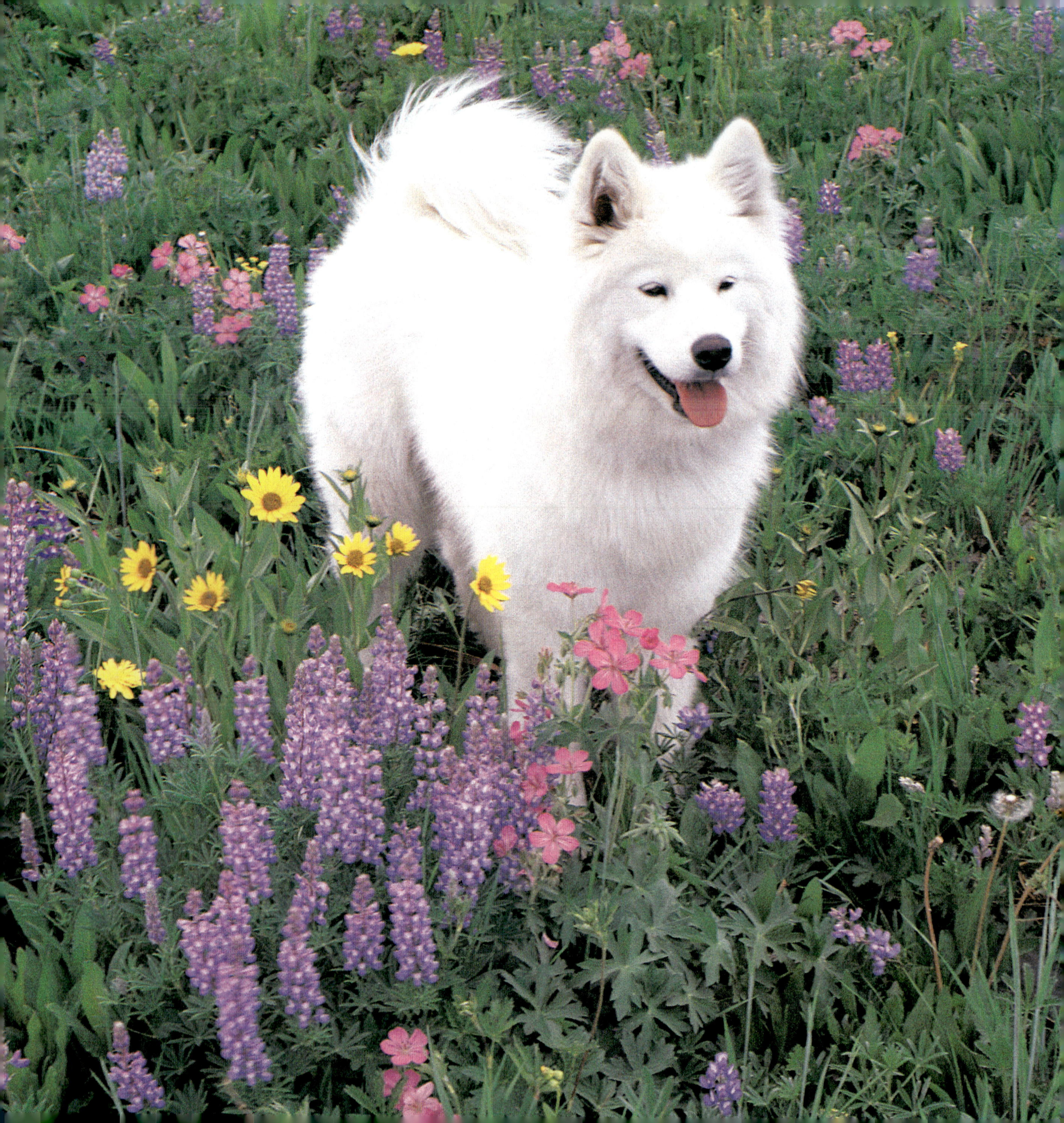

FURTHER READING

American Kennel Club. *The Complete Dog Book.* New York: Howell Book House, 1980.

Bryant, Traphes, and Frances Spatz Leighton. *Dog Days at the White House.* New York: Macmillan Publishing Company, 1975.

Caras, Roger A. *The Roger Caras Pet Book.* New York: Holt, Rinehart and Winston, 1976.

Caras, Roger A. *Roger Caras' Treasury of Great Dog Stories.* New York: Galahad Books, 1987.

Carleson, Delbert G., and James M. Griffin. *Dog Owner's Home Veterinary Handbook.* New York: Howell Book House, 1980.

Carter, Gordon. *Willing Walkers: The Story of Dogs for the Blind.* New York: Abelard-Schuman, 1965.

Cohen, Daniel. *The Encyclopedia of Ghosts.* New York: Dorset, 1984.

Cole, William, ed. *Good Dog Poems.* New York: Charles Scribner's Sons, 1981.

Curtis, Patricia. *Cindy, A Hearing Ear Dog.* New York: E.P. Dutton, 1981.

Dog Fancy magazine. Fancy Publications, Inc. Three Burroughs, Irvine, CA 92718.

Dog World magazine. MacLean Hunter Publishing Corporation, 29 North Wacker Drive, Chicago, IL 60606-3298.

Dougherty, John and Judy. *Dog Trivia.* Boston: Quinlan Press, 1985.

Evans, Job Michael. *The Evans Guide for Civilized City Canines.* New York: Howell Book House, 1988.

Fox, Michael. *Understanding Your Dog.* New York: Bantam Books, 1974.

McLoughlin, John C. *The Canine Clan: A New Look at Man's Best Friend.* New York: The Viking Press, 1983.

Mery, Fernand. *The Dog.* London: Cassell & Company, 1968.

Miller, Gustavus Hindman. *10,000 Dreams Interpreted.* New York: Bell Publishing, 1988.

Morris, Desmond. *Dogwatching.* New York: Crown Publishers, 1986.

Olsen, Stanley J. *Origins of the Domestic Dog.* Tuscon, AZ: University of Arizona Press, 1985.

Porter, Valerie. *The Guinness Book of Almost Everything You Didn't Need to Know About Dogs.* London: Guinness Superlatives, 1986.

Randolph, Mary. *Dog Law.* Berkeley, CA: Nolo Press, 1988.

Riddle, Maxwell. *Dogs Through History.* Fairfax, VA: Denlinger's, 1987.

Robins, Joyce. *The New Complete Book of the Dog.* New York: Gallery Books, 1990.

Silverman, Ruth. *The Dog Observed: Photographs, 1844-1988.* New York: Howell Book House, 1984.

Varner, John and Jeannette. *Dogs of the Conquest.* Norman, OK: University of Oklahoma Press, 1983.

Wylder, Joseph. *The Secret Life of Animals: Psychic Pets.* New York: Bonanza Books, 1978.

• Opposite: Samoyed.

APPENDIX

Animal Advocates

American Dog Owners Association
1654 Columbia Turnpike
Castleton, NY 12033

American Humane Association
63 Inverness Drive East
Englewood, CO 80112

Animal Protection Institute of America
P.O. Box 22505
Sacramento, CA 95810

ASPCA
424 East 92nd Street
New York, NY 10028

Friends of Animals
1841 Broadway
New York, NY 10023

Humane Society of the United States
2100 L Street, NW
Washington, DC 20037

Lost Dogs' Home/Animal Welfare League of
 Victoria
2 Gracie Street
North Melbourne, Victoria 3051
Australia

Royal Social for the Prevention of Cruelty to
 Animals
The Causeway, Horsham
West Sussex RH12 1HG
England

RSPCA
201 Rockwood Road
Yagoona, New South Wales
2000 Australia

RSPCA of Western Australia
P.O. Box 201
Victorian Park 6100
Australia

Toronto Humane Society
11 River Street
Toronto, Ontario
M5A 4CT

World Society for Protection of Animals
P.O. Box 365
Canterbury, Victoria 3126
Australia

INDEX

A
Affenpinscher, 104
Afghan Hound, 24, *103*, 104
Aggressive behavior, 73
Akita, 104
Altering, 72, 82–83, 92–93
American Kennel Club, 102
American Working Terrier Association, 54
Aristotle, 37–38
Assistance dogs, 58–61, *58*, 84

B
Barking and howling, 17, 74
Basenji, 18, 105, *105*
Basset Hound, 102, 105, *105*
Beagle, *80*, 105, *105*
Beds for dogs, 98–99
Belgian Sheepdogs, 106
Bernese Mountain Dog, 106, *106*
Bloodhound, 21, 31, 38, 48, 69, 106
Borzoi, 24, 106
Bouvier de Flandres, 55, 107, *107*
Boxer, 107, *107*
Breeding, 83–84
  breeding clubs, 34
Briard, 107
Brussels Griffon, 107, *107*
Bulldog, 21, 33, 102, 108, *108*
Bush Dog, 18

C
Call of the Wild, The (London), 42
Camp Gone-to-the-Dogs, 99
Canadian Kennel Club, 102
Canidae, family of, 12, 14–16, 22
Canine Companions for Independence, 59, 60
Cape Hunting Dogs, 13, 15, *15*, 16–18, *16–17*
Cat
  common ancestry with dogs, 12
  Egyptians and, 27
  hunting habits, 15
Cerebus, 47
Chihuahua, 21, 59, 102, 108
Chinese Crested Dog, 108 *108*
Chinese Shar-Pei, 69, 110, *111*
Chocolate, effect on dogs, 72
Chow Chow, 29, 50, 108, 110
Collie, 24, 52, 59, 110, *110*
  Bearded, 105
  Border, 106
Coyote, 20
Cynocephali, 45

D
Dachshund, 16, 47, *47*, 69, 73, 102, 110
Dalmation, *8*, 27, *111*, 112
Descartes, René, 39
Dhole (wild dog), 15, 18
Dickens, Charles, 41
Digging behavior, 73
Dingo, 18, *18*, 24
Doberman, 55, 57, 60, 112
Dog accessories, 99
Dog, anatomy of the, 63–64, *64*
  toes and claws, 64

Dog, evolution of the, 12–13
Dog, history of the
  Aztecs, 27, 49
  China, 29
  domestication of, 23
  Egypt, 27
  Europe, medieval, 30–31
  Europe, Renaissance, 33
  Greece and Rome (ancient), 28
  Mesopotamia, 26, *29*
  Persia (ancient), 28, 29
  Renaissance, 33
  Mexico, 26–27
  Plains Indians, 26, *26*
Dog bowls, 99
Dog Fancy magazine, 46, 55
Dog houses, 98, 99
Dog laws, 84–85, 89
  leash laws, 85
  licensing, 85
  traveling restrictions, 89
Dog Museum (St. Louis, Missouri), 46, 52
Dog stars, 52
Dog training, 70–72, 80–81
Dog World magazine, 46, 55
Doggerel, 38, 39
Dogs, beliefs about
  Belgium, 49
  Celts (ancient), 30
  China, 48
  Egypt (ancient), 20, 27
  in dreams, 48–49
  ghost dogs, 49–50
  Greenland, 48
  Iceland, 48

INDEX
125

Ireland, 49
Japan, 29
Medieval Europe, 48
Menominee Indians, 48
in myth and legend, 47–50
Navaho Indians, 20
Persia *ancient), 29, 48
Rome (ancient), 47
Shawnee Indians, 48
South America, 49
worship of, 47
Dogs, communication with, 73–74
Dogs, cruelty to, 89
D.O.G.S. for the Handicapped, 60
Dogs, health problems
  allergies, 95
  bloat, 95
  diabetes, 95
  epilepsy, 95
  heat stroke, 95
  hip dysplasia, 95
  hot spots, 95–96
  pancreatitis, 96
  Parasites, 93–94
  treatment, 96–97
Dogs, in art, 44–46, 44
  Asia, 44
  Greece and Rome (ancient, 44
  medieval Europe, 44–45
Dogs, in church architecture, 30
Dogs, in insignia and coat of arms, 46, 46
Dogs, in literature, 37–43
Dogs, psychic, 50–51
Dogue de Bordeaux, 112
Domestic dog
  classification of, 9, 12, 14
  evolution of, 12–13
  object of scorn, 9, 30, 38

oldest record of, 11
origin of, 26
as pet, 34, 40, 72, 80
as work animal, 30
Draft dogs, 54–55, 103

E

Ears, cropping of, 65–66
Eating and drinking, 66
  feeding dogs, 71–72
Elderly dogs, care of, 97
Eskimo dogs, 26, 104
Euthanasia, 98
Exercise, *34–35*

F

Fever dogs, 48
Finnish Spitz, 112
Fireside Book of Dog Stories, The (Thurber), 42
Florian, 39
Fox, 13, 15, 19
  Arctic Fox, 15
  Fennec, 19
  Kit Fox, 15
  North American Gray Fox, 19
  Red Fox, *19*
Foxhound, 112
Fur and shedding, 65

G

Gazehound, 24, 31
German Shepherd, 17, 52, 55, *55*, 57, 58, *59*, 63, 69, 79, 113

Gnawing and chewing, 80
Great Dane, 52, 102, 113
Greyhound, 27, 53, 113
  Italian, 114
Groenendael puppy, 106
Grooming, 94
Guard dogs, 103
Guide dogs. *See* Assistance dogs.

H

Handicapped persons, dogs for, 60
Health certificates, 89
Hearing, sense of, 68
Homer, 37
Hound of the Baskervilles (Doyle), 49, *49*
Hounds in general, 103
  See also specific breeds.
Humane Societies, 33–34
Hunting dogs, 31, 33, 42, 53, *53*
Huntsman on Foot and Hounds (Ben Marshall), *33*
Husky, 24, 54
  Siberian, 120, *120*

I

Ibizan Hound, 113
Incredible Journey, The (Burnford), 51
Iran (fossil site), *12*
Iraq (fossil site), 11
Islam, attitude toward dogs, 29

J

Jackals, 13, 15, 20, *20*
Japanese Chin, 114

K

Keeshond, 114
Kennel Club (Britain), 34
Komondor, 115, *115*
Kuvasz, 115

L

La Fontaine, Jean, 38
Lamartine, Alphonse de, 40
Lassie Come-Home, 51
Lassie, 52
Law-enforcement dogs, 55, *55*
Lhasa Apso, 115
London, Jack, 42

M

Malamute, *10*, 21, 24, 54, 55, *84*, 97
  Alaska, 104, *104*
Maltese, 33, 115
Maned Wolf, 20
Mastiff, 16, 28, 31, 33, 38, 102, 116
Mating habits, 76
Maturation of dogs, 81
Military dogs, 56, *56*
Milne, A.A., 40
Miniature Pinscher, 116
Mixed breed, *39*
Montaigne, Michel de, *39*
Mushing magazine, 55

N

Neoteny, 17
Neutering. *See* Altering.
Newfoundland, 41, *41*, 54, 59, 116
Newfoundland Club of America, 54
Norwegian Elkhound, 24, 116

O

Old English Sheepdog, 116
Old Yeller, 43, *43*, 52
Overpopulations of dogs, 82–83

P

"Pai Dogs," 29
Papillon, 33, 116, *116*
Parasites
  external, 93
  ticks, *93*
  internal, 94
  worms, 94
Pariah Dog, 24, 29
Pasteur, Louis, 34
Paul Winter Consort, 68
Peat Dog, 24
Pekingese, 29, 63, 116
Performing dogs. *See* Dog stars.
Pharaoh Hound, 117
Phu Quoc dog, 18
Pit Bull. *See* Terrier, American Staffordshire.
Play, signals, for, 79
Pointer, 33, *53*, 103
Polar dog, 24
Police dogs. *See* Law-enforcement dogs.
Pomeranian, 21, 41, 117, *117*
Poodle, *14*, 41, 102, 117, *117*
Pug, 29, 33, 67, 117
Puli, 117
Puppy development, 77, 78–81, *78*, 94
  socialization, 78–79
  teething, 80
Puppy mills, 83
Pyrenean Mountain Dog, 57

R

Rabies, 34, 38
Raccoon Dog, 19
Reproduction, 76–77
Retriever, 31, 103
  Chesapeake Bay, 103
  Flat-Coated, 112
  Golden, *38*, 57, *95*, 113, *113*
    Labrador, *43*, *51*, 55, 57, 59, *61*, 115, *115*
  swimming, fondness for, 18
Rhodesian Ridgeback, 118, *118*
Rin Tin Tin, 52
Rottweiler, 54, 44, 118, *118*
Rousseau, Jean-Jacques, 41

S

Saint Hubert Hound, 31
Salem witch trials, 49
Saluki, 24, 118
Samoyed, 24, *25*, 52, *65*, 119, *122*
Shipperke, 119
Schnauzer, 119
Scott, Walter, 40
Search and rescue dogs, 57
Secret Life of Animals, The (Wilder), 51
Seeing eye dogs. *See* Assistance dogs.
Setter, 31, 33, 113
Sheepdog, 15, *27*, 33
Shepherd dog, 54
  Australian, 105
  Great Pyrenees, *54*, 113
Shetland Sheepdog, 119, *119*
Shih Tzu, 29, 119
Show dogs, 66
Signal dogs, 59
Sled dogs, *40–41*, 54–55, 103
"Sleeve dogs," 29

Smell, sense of
  marking of territory, 75
  sniffing behavior, 75
  See also Sniffer dogs.
Smith, Owen, 53
Sniffer dogs, 57
Society for the Prevention of Cruelty to Animals, 33
Spaniel, 103
  American Water, 103
  Brittany, 107
  Cavalier King Charles, 108
  Clumber, 110
  Cocker, 14, 36, 41, 110, 111
  Irish Water, 114
  Springer, 55
Spaying. See Altering.
Spits, Sr., Carl "Papa," 70
Spitz dog, 24, 27
St. Bernard, 54, 57, 57, 102
Submissive behavior, 73–74

T

Tail, docking of, 65–66
Tail behavior, 75
Taxonomy, science of, 14
Terhune, Albert Payson, 49–50
Terrier, 15, 19, 31, 54, 103
  Airedale, 55, 104
  American Staffordshire, 88, 105
  Bedlington, 105
  Boston, 107
  Bull, 33
  Cairn, 108, 109
  Dandie Dinmont, 112
  Fox, 112, 113
  Jack Russell, 32, 114, 114
  Kerry Blue, 115
  Manchester, 115
  Scottish, 119, 119
  Skye, 120
  West Highland White, 90, 120
  Yorkshire, 62, 73, 102, 121, 121
The Selection Hygiene and Illnesses of the Dog (Turberville), 39
Therapy Dogs International, 60
Thin Man, The, 52, 52
Touch, sense of, 66
Traveling with dogs, 89

U

United Kennel Club, 102

V

Vaccinations, 92
Vest, George Graham, 43, 53, 91
Veterinarians, choosing, 91
Veterinary medicine, 34, 92–94, 95–98, 95
Vision, sense of, 66–67
Vizsla, 120

W

War, dogs and, 28
  See also Military dogs.
Weimaraner dog, 46, 55, 100, 103, 120
Welsh Corgi, 120
Werewolf lore, 9, 24, 24, 30
Whippet, 24, 120, 120
Wild dog
  definition of, 16
  differences from domestic, 17
Wolf
  as ancestors of dogs, 14
  Asiatic, 21
  domestication of, 23
  evolution of, 13–14
  extinction of, 24
  hunting habits, 21
  legends and myths, 25
  northern wolf, 15
  Timber Wolf, 21
  wooden figurehead (Florida), 13
Wolfhound, 31
  Irish, 102, 102, 114

X

Xoloitzcuintli, 121